CD-CEM-657

TO ALLEN WHEELIS
WHOSE VISION HAS BEEN
OUR LIFELONG INSPIRATION

TABLE OF CONTENTS

LIST OF ILLUSTRATIONS

ACKNOWLEDGEMENTS

Our heartfelt appreciation goes to our families and close friends who encouraged, supported and inspired our work. To: Ada and Stuart Weisser, Larry and Gertrude Wolf, Frieda and Paul Schwartz, Marilyn Orenstein, Nancy, Phil and Michael Kawesch, Audrey and Stephen Knippa, Laura and David Mills, Sally and Sam Ferris, Catherine McNally, Jim McMahon, Natalie Vale, Lorraine Altman and Betty Leyerle.

Our gratitude goes to all the people we interviewed in shopping malls in California and New York and in our Odd Couple Workshops, who shared their time, thoughts and feelings with us. Their interest and cooperation during the various stages of our research was indispensable.

We wish to acknowledge our debt to all the psychologists, neuroscientists and researchers with special thanks to Drs. Roger Sperry and Joseph Bogen. It was their contributions to the study of brain lateralization that built the foundation for our theory of the Odd Couple Syndrome.

And, of course, our thanks to the brilliant and insightful Neil Simon who created the great American folk heroes, Felix and Oscar, and provided us with the perfect title for our book.

Introduction

Are you very neat or very sloppy?

Do others criticize you for it?

How does it affect your personal relationships?

Are you a Felix Unger or an Oscar Madison? In Neil Simon's story, the styles of the neat and sloppy person were clearly drawn. Here at last was a true, though exaggerated, picture of the everyday interaction between two people, one excessively neat, the other hopelessly sloppy.

When we began this study of neatness and sloppiness, we were amazed to discover how little scientific work had been directed toward demystifying these most common forms of human behavior. When exploration of the existing material on the subject was of little avail, we embarked on a personal search for answers. A hunch that there was a link between the craftsman/artist and the neat/sloppy phenomenon led to the examination of the body of work known as Split-Brain research.

The theory behind the Odd Couple Syndrome is based on the hypothesis that neatness and sloppiness are profoundly influenced by a favored left-hemisphere or right-hemisphere style of perception. Most brain researchers believe that each hemisphere of the cerebral cortex has its own separate and private perceptions and its own impulses to act. The left brain specializes in rational, organized and sequential

1

thought, while the right brain thinks in emotional, intuitive and spatial terms.

We maintain that it is not *attitude*, as many believe, that creates the dichotomy between Neat and Sloppy, but *perception*. It is not a neurotic fixation, but rather that people experience the same reality through two different perspectives. With this comes the left-brain dominant tendency to be neat and the right-brain dominant tendency to be sloppy. We would, however, like to clarify the use of the terms "neat" and "sloppy" within the context of this book. We are aware that they often carry a negative image . "Neatnik" and "slob" are terms which imply a quality of poor character and are often delivered with an air of superiority. This study's use of "neat" and "sloppy," however, implies no judgment. Neat is neither better nor worse than sloppy; it is different. We find the terms appropriate in spite of their "moral" connotations precisely because there is a popular concensus regarding their implications. That agreed meaning coincides closely with our own definition.

Neatness and Sloppiness are those forms of behavior which relate to how one deals with his material environment. It is the difference between the Neat and the Sloppy, that is, the dominance of the one orientation over the other, that dictates the style by which one classifies, organizes, arranges, uses, maintains and cares for his material objects.

The hundreds of individuals who have attended our experiential workshops having accepted the above non-judgmental theory have had little trouble defining themselves as neat or sloppy when filling out questionnaires and participating in group exercises.

Nevertheless, the clash between the Neat and the Sloppy is real and widespread. Each sees the world in a different way and each follows the dictate of his own perceptions. Herein lies the Neat/Sloppy dilemma. This book is for and about all of us. It goes to the heart of the unspoken and seldom acknowledged parts of ourselves. We hope you will find it enlightening, amusing and liberating, and that it will serve to deepen the quality of your self-acceptance.

Chapter 1
The Odd Couple

Neat/Sloppy behavior is a thread which weaves its way through the intricate fabric of everyday life, from the attention we give to our appearance and our possessions to the way we work and play. The clash between them has been experienced with humor as well as with exasperation. It is the inexplicable raw material of human interaction.

In the spring of 1979, Max Weisser and I were asked to write and produce a satire for a convention of the Association of Humanistic Psychology. At that time, I was constantly irritated by my eighteen-year-old son's idea of shared housekeeping. In an attempt to retain my sanity and release some of my frustrations, we included a short sketch in the play about the Neat/Sloppy dilemma.

The play is entitled "Peter Faces Life in a Higher Consciousness Shopping Center." It's about a young man distressed by the conditions in the world who searches (or shops) for the meaning of life.

In one scene, Peter meets a wise old sage and asks him why the world is in such a mess. This precipitates a discussion in which the old man offers his experience and a solution:

"I have always been concerned about social injustice. When I was a young man I thought that all the human suffering I saw around me was caused by Capitalism. The problem was that the world was split between the rich and the poor. So I became a

Marxist and worked to bring about a social revolution. But after many years of personal sacrifice and struggle, I realized that that was not the answer.

"At this point I became keenly aware of the insidious nature of racism and how the anger between black and white poisoned human relations and made cooperative social reform impossible. So I joined the civil rights movement and worked for school and housing integration. But after years of dedication, I realized that that was not the answer either.

"Just about that time I discovered the all-pervasive nature of sexism. I realized that our society was paying a high price in unhappy relationships as a result of centuries of suppression of women's rights. So I joined consciousness-raising groups and participated in demonstrations for the Equal Rights Amendment. As time passed I realized this too, was only a small part of the answer to what tormented mankind.

"Then I was introduced to Eastern Religion and for the first time began to understand the true nature of the human condition. I learned to meditate and make contact with the universal essence. I could now see that human suffering was the result of man's attachment to the material world, and that only through the attainment of enlightenment could social harmony be achieved. Then I had a flash of cosmic insight.

"Enlightenment was not the answer. The answer was so simple. It had been with me for most of my life. Humanity's inability to live in peace grew out of a basic irreconcilable difference between people. I realized there are really only two kinds of people in the world, the Neat and the Sloppy."

"Peter, you say the world is a mess, but who do you think messed it up? The Sloppy People! The Neat people are always fixing the things the Sloppy people break, finding things that Sloppy people lose and cleaning the dishes that Sloppy people leave in the sink!

"Ah, Peter, you might ask, how do Sloppy people get that way? Well, the psychologists say Sloppy people are victims of an anal fixation, but that is based on a discredited theory. The latest research, which was done at Pristine University by Wilbur

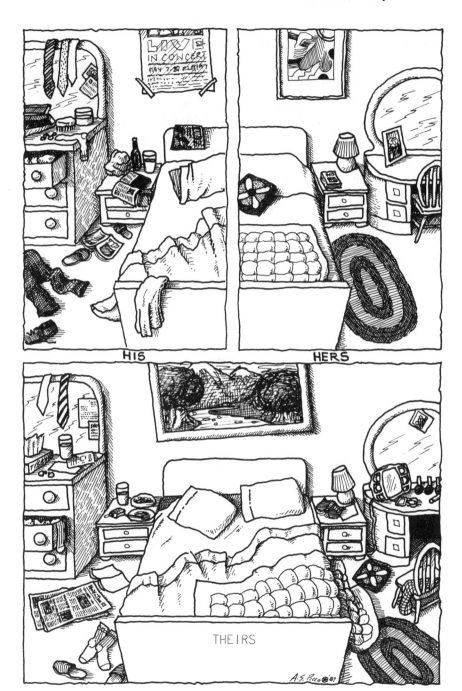

WHEN NEAT AND SLOPPY COLLIDE SLOPPY PREVAILS

Watson, who discovered DNE, has turned up some startling information. He has isolated two new genes, a sloppy gene and a neat gene! But the bad news is that the sloppy gene is dominant. Some people have suggested political solutions. The conservatives say we must restrict the sloppies' employment and keep them out of the suburbs. The liberals say that they need understanding, education, and besides that, there is no such thing as a sloppy person. I think both solutions are extreme. My solution is to find a homeland for the sloppy people.''

Our purpose in presenting this part of the play was to express the view that Neat and Sloppy have a serious but unrecognized place in the scheme of things. From the enthusiastic response, we knew we had struck a highly resonant, emotional chord. Several members of the audience approached us to share their feelings about a Neat or Sloppy mate.

We decided this matter deserved further consideration. What is this all about? Does anyone know? Where can one look for answers? We needed to get to the core of it. We conferred with friends and colleagues who specialize in psychology, sociology, anthropology, biology, and education. We found no one with a grip on the internal dynamics of the Neat/Sloppy theme.

Even the Greek tragedians had missed the theme of Neat/Sloppy because of their preoccupation with greed, lust, and pride, but one contemporary American dramatist did not.

When ''The Odd Couple'' opened on Broadway in 1964, it was greeted with wide public acclaim. The brilliant comic playwright Neil Simon had touched a familiar chord in his audience which had long been unacknowledged and undefined.

Up until this time, the assumption that neatness was the ideal way of life had seldom been challenged. But this story of two divorced men with opposing life-styles sharing an apartment reversed the popular notion of ''the Sloppy'' as the incompetent and ''the Neat'' as the effective one. Felix Unger is thrown out of his home by his wife because of his incessant, compulsive cleaning and cooking, only to repeat the same pattern with his new roommate, Oscar Madison, who is forever on the verge of throwing him out. Felix, the photographer, interior decorator, and gourmet cook, is perpetually cleaning, planning,

and trying to control everything and everyone in sight. Oscar responds with irritation and resistance. Felix's intentions are generally frustrated, which lead him to suffer anxiety and an assortment of physical symptoms.

Oscar, the sportswriter, card player, and womanizer, is the neat person's living nightmare—a human catastrophe. He can, within a few minutes after arrival, transform the immaculate living room into the aftermath of a tornado. Like Charles Schulz's Pig Pen he moves in a cloud of filth. He drowns Felix's gourmet meals in ketchup and keeps his bedroom looking like a demolition site. His personality, however, is warm, relaxed and jovial, and he is liked by everyone. It is not surprising that "The Odd Couple" has enjoyed lengthy theatre, movie, and television runs and has entered into the realm of popular folklore. Apparently, there is a Felix or Oscar in all of us.

Inspired by Neil Simon's play and our own subsequent excursions into theatrical comedy, we discovered the link between the Neat/Sloppy pattern and a myriad of other polarized behavioral styles that comprise the spectrum of human personality. Careful observation and research into the "Odd Couple Syndrome" has not only helped solve an interesting mystery, but has forged a key to unlock a new window into the human mind as well.

Before going into the substance of the research that led us to develop our Odd Couple theory, we thought it would give the reader a better overview of the subject if we could recreate the proceedings of an actual workshop.

What follows is the edited transcript of our presentation at the New York State Personnel and Guidance Counselors Convention in November of 1984.

Chapter 2
NYSPGC Convention

Welcome to the Odd Couple Syndrome workshop. My name is Selwyn Mills and this is my associate Max Weisser. We are both psychotherapists from Great Neck, N.Y. who have been conducting Neat/Sloppy workshops for the past three years.

Earlier this morning a colleague of mine who formally attended one of our Odd Couple seminars handed me a poem which he asked me to share with the group. It reads:

BLESS THIS MESS
THE SINK IS FILLED WITH DISHES
THE SILVERWARE IS TURNING GREEN
MY BEDROOM COULD MAKE A COCKROACH SCREAM
UNDERNEATH THE NEWSPAPERS IF YOU GIVE A TUG
YOU'LL SHOCKINGLY DISCOVER
THE FLOOR DOES HAVE A RUG
IF YOU ARE IN MY BATHROOM
BE CAREFUL ALL AROUND
IT'S SAFE ENOUGH TO WASH YOUR FACE
BUT HEAVENS DON'T SIT DOWN
THIS PLACE IS GETTING OUT OF HAND

THOUGH I TRY MY VERY BEST
I VOW AGAIN TO KEEP IT NEAT
BUT MEANWHILE PLEASE
BLESS THIS MESS

Which reminds me of my son David. In his bedroom everything he owned, used, and discarded was piled on his bed, the counters, window sills and floor, on every horizontal surface that was available. In fact, when the telephone rang in his room, it could take a considerable time to locate the phone. When he went to sleep he had to sweep everything off the bed. There was a lot of hassling back and forth between us but for the most part he confined the mess to his own room. One day upon returning home to my apartment, I was surprised to find that my son had come into my personal bathroom, unscrewed the toothpaste, squeezed it on the sink, left the cap off and scotch-taped an inscribed index card on the mirror for me to see. It read: ''When neat and sloppy clash, sloppy prevails.'' He had a point!

Our interest in pursuing the psychological roots of the Neat/Sloppy phenomenon was sparked when Max and I were invited to write a satirical play for a psychological conference.

It was called ''Peter Faces Life in the Higher Consciousness Shopping Center.''

One of the humorous scenes dealt with neatness and sloppiness. After the performance and for months after that people who had seen the play approached me and said, ''Selwyn, that piece you did on neat and sloppy is so true! My wife this...My daughter that...My son is...'' There was so much passion around the whole idea of neatness and sloppiness that we realized that we were not alone in our thinking about the issue. Other people were as concerned with neat/sloppy implications as we were. What was the basis for the strong reaction by the audience? We decided to do some research on the matter and reexamined the Freudian theory. Freud was the only one who dealt with the issue of neatness and sloppiness. He thought that the nature of parental toilet training caused the child to become anal retentive or expulsive. However, this was about seventy years ago and since then many of Freud's ideas have been disproven. His theory just didn't explain the dynamics of neatness and sloppiness.

So, here we are...! left with the question of what is behind neatness and sloppiness. Why are some people sloppy and some people neat? What is it all about?

As a result of our research we came up with something that we're going to discuss here today, but not before we get into some experiential exercises. Our intention is to involve you in what your concerns are regarding neatness and sloppiness.

I would like all the neat people to go to one side of the room and the sloppy people to go to the other side of the room. You will notice that the group has split almost exactly in half. It is no longer a surprise to us when this 50/50 breakdown occurs since we have come to believe that neats and sloppies are evenly divided in the population.

People are pretty honest about their neatness and sloppiness. However, if you ask a person, "How are you in bed?" (laughter), they are not always honest, especially in a room of strangers. Then the response is usually "terrific." Or if you ask a person, "Do you have a good sense of humor?" everyone says, "Ah, terrific!" But if you ask people, "Are you neat or sloppy?" they are pretty honest and say, "Yeah, I'm kind of on the sloppy side—sometimes I think I'm a real Oscar Madison "

Okay, now I'd like each neat person to pick a sloppy person and sit in a dyad. Neat people are to talk about three things you *like* about being neat and three things you *don't like* about being neat. Following that, the other person is to give three things they *like* about being sloppy and three things they *don't like* about being sloppy. Now take about fifteen minutes to share that information with each other and then each of you can explore the effect those qualities have on your personal life...Now let's reconvene as a single group.

I see another person joining us late. Your name is Dorothy?

Dorothy, the group has been discussing the matter of being neat or sloppy. In which category would you put yourself? Sloppy? Good, we are short one sloppy. Dorothy, before you came in we were discussing what we liked about being neat or sloppy and what we didn't like about being neat or sloppy. Since you describe yourself as sloppy, would you like to tell us what you like about being sloppy?

> " I'm not in the habit of putting things away. I like the freedom it gives me. I don't feel compelled to keep things in order so I'm more relaxed. "

And how does being sloppy interfere with your life?

> " I can never find my keys; I'm impatient about filing my bills, tax information, etc. so I end up with several folders for the same subject. "

READER STOP NOW!

Before you read further, consider filling out the enclosed questions.
Their completion may serve the following purposes:

1. Give you a key to your own personal neat/sloppy style.
2. Passed along to friends, it will help them determine their pattern.
3. Filled out jointly with your spouse, lover, roommate, it will pinpoint the areas of harmony and conflict.

When answering the questions, consider your responses carefully and avoid the "Sometimes" column whenever possible. If the questionnaire is filled out jointly, have the first person mark the box of choice with a horizontal dash, then read aloud the statements to the second respondant (this avoids the other person being influenced by your responses). Those responses can be marked with a vertical line in the boxes of choice. This will clearly show the places where the couple is the same (the horizontal and vertical marks will cross). Where the marks are at opposite ends of the columns, Always/Never indicates the differences.

When these worksheets are completed, put them aside in a safe place. Later on in the book you will find another type of self-evaluation test which will help you define your own perceptual style from a different perspective.

See Illustration #1

```
+-----------------------------+        +---------------------------+
|   ODD COUPLE SYNDROME       |        |  MILLS/WEISSER            |
|   QUESTIONNAIRE             |        |  GREAT NECK N.Y.          |
+-----------------------------+        +---------------------------+
```

NAME_____

	ALWAYS	OFTEN	SOMETIMES	RARELY	NEVER
1. I take good care of my possessions.					
2. My decisions are more spontaneous than deliberate.					
3. In my home I keep things well organized					
4. I make concrete plans for the future					
5. When I solve problems I take a playful rather than a business-like approach.					
6. I pay my bills on time.					
7. I tend to smoke, drink or eat too much.					
8. I consider myself a saver rather than a thrower.					
9. I am late for appointments.					
1o. I have trouble keeping my personal papers up to date.					
11. I squeeze a tube of toothpaste from the bottom and replace the cap.					
12. I am a careful craftsman.					
13. I rely on my intuition in assessing new people					
14. When I work on a project I plan things in detail.					
15. I find keeping order a bother but do it promptly anyway.					
16. I have trouble finding my keys.					
17. When I start a task I follow through.					
18. I consider myself self-disciplined.					
19. I consider hunches very important in making decisions.					
20. I am very concerned about my physical appearance.					
21. On vacations, I enjoy spur-of-the-moment activities rather than set plans.					
22. I am impelled to find specific places to put things.					
23. I have a strong feeling to get up and move around when at a lecture or movie.					
24. After planning my day I resist intrusions that would put me off track.					

```
+------------------------------------------------+
| RATE YOURSELF ON THE FOLLOWING SCALE           |
| VERY NEAT   O O O O O   VERY SLOPPY            |
|             1 2 3 4 5                           |
+------------------------------------------------+
```

MALE_____
FEMALE

Illustration #1

ODD COUPLE SYNDROME
QUESTIONNAIRE

MILLS/WEISSER
GREAT NECK N.Y.

NAME_____

	ALWAYS	OFTEN	SOMETIMES	RARELY	NEVER
1. I take good care of my possessions.					
2. My decisions are more spontaneous than deliberate.					
3. In my home I keep things well organized					
4. I make concrete plans for the future					
5. When I solve problems I take a playful rather than a business-like approach.					
6. I pay my bills on time.					
7. I tend to smoke, drink or eat too much.					
8. I consider myself a saver rather than a thrower.					
9. I am late for appointments.					
1o. I have trouble keeping my personal papers up to date.					
11. I squeeze a tube of toothpaste from the bottom and replace the cap.					
12. I am a careful craftsman.					
13. I rely on my intuition in assessing new people					
14. When I work on a project I plan things in detail.					
15. I find keeping order a bother but do it promptly anyway.					
16. I have trouble finding my keys.					
17. When I start a task I follow through.					
18. I consider myself self-disciplined.					
19. I consider hunches very important in making decisions.					
20. I am very concerned about my physical appearance.					
21. On vacations, I enjoy spur-of-the-moment activities rather than set plans.					
22. I am impelled to find specific places to put things.					
23. I have a strong feeling to get up and move around when at a lecture or movie.					
24. After planning my day I resist intrusions that would put me off track.					

RATE YOURSELF ON THE FOLLOWING SCALE

VERY NEAT   O O O O O   VERY SLOPPY
            1 2 3 4 5

MALE_____
FEMALE

Illustration #1

15 THE ODD COUPLE SYNDROME

```
ODD COUPLE SYNDROME
QUESTIONNAIRE
```

```
MILLS/WEISSER
GREAT NECK N.Y.
```

NAME_____

	ALWAYS	OFTEN	SOMETIMES	RARELY	NEVER
1. I take good care of my possessions.					
2. My decisions are more spontaneous than deliberate.					
3. In my home I keep things well organized					
4. I make concrete plans for the future					
5. When I solve problems I take a playful rather than a business-like approach.					
6. I pay my bills on time.					
7. I tend to smoke, drink or eat too much.					
8. I consider myself a saver rather than a thrower.					
9. I am late for appointments.					
1o. I have trouble keeping my personal papers up to.date.					
11. I squeeze a tube of toothpaste from the bottom and replace the cap.					
12. I am a careful craftsman.					
13. I rely on my intuition in assessing new people					
14. When I work on a project I plan things in detail.					
15. I find keeping order a bother but do it promptly anyway.					
16. I have trouble finding my keys.					
17. When I start a task I follow through.					
18. I consider myself self-disciplined.					
19. I consider hunches very important in making decisions.					
20. I am very concerned about my physical appearance.					
21. On vacations, I enjoy spur-of-the-moment activities rather than set plans.					
22. I am impelled to find specific places to put things.					
23. I have a strong feeling to get up and move around when at a lecture or movie.					
24. After planning my day I resist intrusions that would put me off track.					

```
RATE YOURSELF ON THE FOLLOWING SCALE
VERY NEAT  O O O O O  VERY SLOPPY
           1 2 3 4 5
```

MALE_____
FEMALE

Illustration #1

```
┌─────────────────────────────┐        ┌──────────────────┐
│  ODD COUPLE SYNDROME         │        │ MILLS/WEISSER    │
│  QUESTIONNAIRE               │        │ GREAT NECK N.Y.  │
└─────────────────────────────┘        └──────────────────┘
```

NAME_____

	ALWAYS	OFTEN	SOMETIMES	RARELY	NEVER
1. I take good care of my possessions.					
2. My decisions are more spontaneous than deliberate.					
3. In my home I keep things well organized					
4. I make concrete plans for the future					
5. When I solve problems I take a playful rather than a business-like approach.					
6. I pay my bills on time.					
7. I tend to smoke, drink or eat too much.					
8. I consider myself a saver rather than a thrower.					
9. I am late for appointments.					
1o. I have trouble keeping my personal papers up to date.					
11. I squeeze a tube of toothpaste from the bottom and replace the cap.					
12. I am a careful craftsman.					
13. I rely on my intuition in assessing new people					
14. When I work on a project I plan things in detail.					
15. I find keeping order a bother but do it promptly anyway.					
16. I have trouble finding my keys.					
17. When I start a task I follow through.					
18. I consider myself self-disciplined.					
19. I consider hunches very important in making decisions.					
20. I am very concerned about my physical appearance.					
21. On vacations, I enjoy spur-of-the-moment activities rather than set plans.					
22. I am impelled to find specific places to put things.					
23. I have a strong feeling to get up and move around when at a lecture or movie.					
24. After planning my day I resist intrusions that would put me off track.					

```
┌──────────────────────────────────────────────┐
│ RATE YOURSELF ON THE FOLLOWING SCALE           │   MALE_____
│ VERY NEAT  O O O O O  VERY SLOPPY              │   FEMALE
│            1 2 3 4 5                            │
└──────────────────────────────────────────────┘
```

Illustration #1

17 THE ODD COUPLE SYNDROME

```
┌─────────────────────────────┐
│    ODD COUPLE SYNDROME       │        ┌──────────────────┐
│    QUESTIONNAIRE             │        │ MILLS/WEISSER    │
└─────────────────────────────┘        │ GREAT NECK N.Y.  │
                                        └──────────────────┘
```

NAME_____

	ALWAYS	OFTEN	SOMETIMES	RARELY	NEVER

1. I take good care of my possessions.
2. My decisions are more spontaneous than deliberate.
3. In my home I keep things well organized
4. I make concrete plans for the future
5. When I solve problems I take a playful rather than a business-like approach.
6. I pay my bills on time.
7. I tend to smoke, drink or eat too much.
8. I consider myself a saver rather than a thrower.
9. I am late for appointments.
1o. I have trouble keeping my personal papers up to date.
11. I squeeze a tube of toothpaste from the bottom and replace the cap.
12. I am a careful craftsman.
13. I rely on my intuition in assessing new people
14. When I work on a project I plan things in detail.
15. I find keeping order a bother but do it promptly anyway.
16. I have trouble finding my keys.
17. When I start a task I follow through.
18. I consider myself self-disciplined.
19. I consider hunches very important in making decisions.
20. I am very concerned about my physical appearance.
21. On vacations, I enjoy spur-of-the-moment activities rather than set plans.
22. I am impelled to find specific places to put things.
23. I have a strong feeling to get up and move around when at a lecture or movie.
24. After planning my day I resist intrusions that would put me off track.

```
┌────────────────────────────────────────────┐
│ RATE YOURSELF ON THE FOLLOWING SCALE         │      MALE_____
│ VERY NEAT  O O O O O  VERY SLOPPY            │      FEMALE
│            1 2 3 4 5                          │
└────────────────────────────────────────────┘
```

Illustration #1

LET'S RETURN TO THE WORKSHOP NOW

As I said earlier,the issues of Neatness and Sloppiness reflected deeper concerns than appeared on the surface. However, we found that nothing definitive had been done in the field of psychology or in any of the other social sciences to explain these behaviors.

We speculated with various ideas and finally came upon the subject of craftsmen and artists. We realized that craftsmen and artists approach their work in different ways: I am a craftsman, that's my nature—very deliberate; I think out something in advance; I plan it; I get all my materials together and execute it in a kind of structured way. Max is an artist. Artists tend to approach their work in an impulsive, spontaneous, expressive way, starting by doing it and then working with what they have. The initial approach is basically different.

Max and I decided that to test the validity of this idea we would have to encounter artists and craftsmen to find out whether they use different methods. One of the things we noticed about artists and craftsmen was that most craftsmen are Neat and most artists are Sloppy. From my own personal experience, I've noticed that. I've always been very neat and I'm a craftsman. Max is an artist and he tends to be sloppy. We wondered if there was any special meaning in this difference.

Over a period of months we went to art galleries and craft shows. We went to street fairs and interviewed artists and craftsmen. We asked them: "How do you approach your work?" "Are you neat or sloppy?" "What is your home like?" "How do you behave at your work?" By exploring all these subjects, we came up with a very high correlation for artists being sloppy and for craftsmen being neat.

We were one step from making a link with split-brain research.

We had become familiar with split-brain research which had been done back in the 60s. How many people know anything about left and right functioning?...Okay. So we'll review it very quickly.

Back in the early 60's, at the California Institute of Technology, there were some very important operations that were done on epileptic patients. There were twenty-one epileptic patients who had been suffering from incurable epilepsy. Drugs, and other therapy were futile — nothing worked on them. They agreed to subject themselves to experimental operations which were being done by Dr.Joseph Bogen in California. Roger Sperry and Michael Gazzaniga were psychologists who were dealing with this issue as well. These operations had been done on monkeys and cats very successfully. They felt that by severing the corpus callosum, they would stop the seizures that these patients were having. Well, incredibly, the operations were done and every one of the twenty-one patients had reduced seizures. They no longer suffered the same symptoms of epilepsy which many had suffered from all their lives.

Psychologists Roger Sperry (who recently won the Nobel Prize for his work in split-brain research) and Michael Gazzaniga were looking for differences in personality among these patients. It was very difficult to see anything different; on the surface they seemed to function quite well. In order to investigate the matter further, they devised a whole battery of different kinds of tests in which they blocked out one eye and gave information to the other. The left side of the body is controlled by the right side of the brain and the right side of the body is controlled by the left side of the brain. We have known this for many years.

When people had injuries to the left side of the brain, a speech disturbance called aphasia would occur. (This was discovered mainly among soldiers or accident victims.) The early physicians never really understood the consequences on the right side. During the course of these experiments, they discovered some astonishing things about how the left and the right brain functioned in these twenty-one people. They found that the left brain did not know what the right brain was doing and that these people were actually living with two seperate brains. Whereas, most normal people will constantly process back and forth across the corpus callosum, these people were functioning either

out of the left brain or out of the right brain for each process. They tested this out by an ingenious experiment of blocking off the left eye or the right eye and determining how much information was coming into the opposite hemisphere.

You see, the fact that these people had epilepsy had nothing to do with the subsequent discoveries they made. It only gave Sperry and Gazzaniga the opportunity to experiment with people who had a separated left and right hemisphere. So it had nothing to do with epilepsy as such...a normal person will use both left and right brain and will constantly and instantaneously transfer information from left and right.

However, what they discovered from these experiments was that the left and right brain have very specific functions. They're very different.

The left side of the brain was found to be analytic, organized, step-by-step in thinking, detail-conscious, rational, verbal, very time-oriented, had linear thinking and was logical. The right brain thought in images, was sensual, mysterious, abstract, intuitive, timeless, irrational, holistic, simultaneous, inarticulate, had very little speech, had spatial qualities, was disorganized, had a need for immediate gratification, was creative. Lateralization of function is believed to be true for the general population, but there are some exceptions.

Left-handed people processed slightly differently.

Left-handedness has been assessed as being approximately ten percent of the general population. Of this group two thirds are believed to have a hemispheric lateralization similar to that of the right-handed person. That is, logic and sequential thinking on the left side and spatial and intuitive thinking of the right. The other third seem to have their brain functions reversed or equally lateralized. In general, handedness is not a reliable indicator of brain dominance.

During the years that followed the ground-breaking studies done by Sperry and Gazzaniga , many other psychologists and researchers conducted experiments with normal people who had not been epileptics or brain damaged in any way. They found through these experiments that most people seem to have a dominant mode, and would be either left-brain dominant or right-brain dominant. As a result, their personality styles would be very different.

As a result of our study of left/right brain research, we developed our theory of the Odd Couple Syndrome and we were able to determine from this that a person who is left-brain dominant will tend to be neat and a person who is right-brain dominant will tend to be sloppy. When we got a little more deeply into it, we combined it with a theory called NLP, which is Neurolinguistic Programming. I don't know how many of you are familiar with neurolinguistics....

Neurolinguistics deals with the sensory modes—the way in which we take in information. We take in information visually, or audibly, or kinesthetically, or through gustatory, or olfactory means, and we process that in our brain. It is our belief that the person who takes in information visually and processes it in his *left brain*, will be *neat and organized*. If he takes in information visually *and* processes it in his *right brain*, he will be *neat and disorganized*. If he takes in information kinesthetically, that is, takes in information through his feelings— through his senses primarily—he'll be *sloppy and disorganized*. If he takes in information kinesthetically and processes it in his left brain, he'll be *sloppy but organized*.

That is our four-part matrix which pretty much explains 75-80% of the thousand people we tested with questionnaires and interviews.

It is important to point out that there are variations and overlaps within each group. One example would be that of Jack Klugman who played Oscar Madison in the TV series "The Odd Couple."

Brett Somers, Jack's former wife, was asked whether Jack was sloppy in real life. She replied, "Oh, God, yes. One day I walked into our living room where we have an enormous coffee table in the center of the room piled with papers. I asked Jack, "Do you know where the November utility bill is? I don't think we paid it?" Jack walked over to the mess of letters on the table and picked out the item I was looking for." I don't know how he does it."

Apparently within the realm of a right brain kinesthetic person such as Jack Klugman, there is a form of selective organization.

Any questions from the floor?

ED: Is anyone totally one-sided?

What we have to clarify is that almost no one is *exclusively* left or right brained. There is no such thing as a left- or right-brained person unless you never use one hemisphere.

As a matter of fact, when we were meeting with Dr. Joseph Bogen, the original neurosurgeon who did those split-brain operations, he told us the story about a very famous case in the middle of the nineteenth century: A neurosurgeon performed an autopsy on a prominent attorney and found out that the man's right hemisphere was atrophied, that it had almost never been used in his adult life. He had actually lived with one hemisphere—the left hemisphere—all his life. Most people never noticed the difference. Dr. Bogen's comment was: "There are people walking around today who never use their right hemisphere. If they live with just their left hemisphere, they're logical and rational all the time. They express very little emotion and have a flat sense of humor. This type of personality was aptly labeled "Alexithymic" by Dr. Klaus Hoppe, a professor at UCLA. You might call someone like that an "emotional illiterate."

We believe part of this is genetic and part is environmental training. From birth, children tend to prefer one or the other hemisphere; one or the other grows more rapidly and starts taking on more of the processes of living than the other. There are obvious personality expressions of this preference that you'll observe in people as you start to look at them in this context. You'll notice how so many people are coming out of their left brain—or coming out of their right brain—in their initial approach to things. So, as we said before, nobody is strictly a right- or left-brained person unless they're extreme. Most people are somewhere in between with a *preference*.

It's that preference which we believe creates the Neat/Sloppy dilemma. If you process information visually and send that to your left brain, your left brain immediately starts to go to work on categorizing and organizing —step-by-step. It is that kind of processing which creates our perception, creates what we know as neatness—a feeling that everything has to be in order. When things are not in order, the left-brained person gets upset and irritated and just has to "fix things up."

If you process primarily with your right brain where most information is taken in kinesthetically through the senses, through your feelings, well, you just don't notice the details. You know details are there; you see them in a peripheral way, but they're not of prime importance to you, and so, in contrast to the left-brained person who

TURNING WORK INTO PLAY

must "fix things up," you can very easily "pile things up." For example, if you process in your right brain, then this whole jumble in here (points to the right brain on the chart) looks sloppy (laughter). No judgment implied!

As you may notice in this "photograph" of the brain, look how complicated and how mixed up the right brain is. And look how much like a ladder the left brain is (laughter). That's the way it looks through a camera...no, it's not a photograph; it's a drawing — an artist's conception of what the brain looks like. Isn't it a craftsman-like job? (laughter)...They didn't find these ladder marks. No. Those are our conceptions. (General talk and laughter)   See Illustration #2

How does all this relate to how people get along? What we found is that when we ask people to speak from their own experiences about how it has been to live with their opposite type, there's a lot of irritation and resentment, even hostility about how the other person is "dumping" on them. The left-brain person says, "Oh, my wife, she never hangs anything up; she's sloppy about this and that — and she *knows* it irritates me." Or vice versa: The right-brain person says, "She's always directing me, always telling me what to do, always telling me I should do it this way or do it that way, and that time is so important."

So, what we try to do is have people accept the things about one another which actually are a reflection of their perceptual style — that's the way that person IS! They're not doing it to hurt you; they're doing it because that's how they see the world. Essentially there's not going to be much change, but there could be accommodation.

Debbie was talking about her husband who is a little on the sloppy side and leaves all his clothes lying around and they pile up until the room finally is a mess. Now, Debbie says that things are getting better since she spoke to him about it. Accommodation is occurring. It is part of a process I will explain later on in the workshop.

And now we'd like to present two short dramatic skits which we think typify some very common experiences for all of us.

We are fortunate to have with us today two of the stars of the play "Peter Faces Life in the Higher Consciousness Shopping Center" — Sandy Wickham and Lou Mandel — who have agreed to play the roles of Shirley and Bill in the first sketch and Lori and Lew in the second.

LEFT BRAIN   RIGHT BRAIN

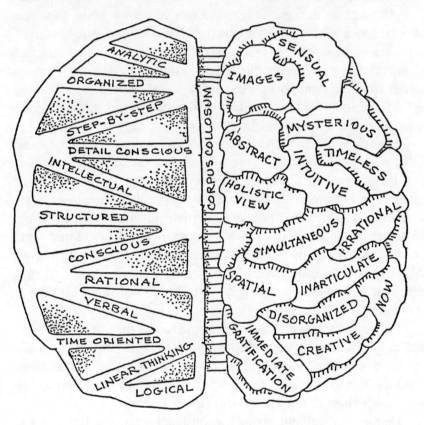

CEREBRAL CORTEX

Illustration #2

Bill and Shirley are preparing to go out for the evening. Bill is putting the finishing brush strokes to his hair.

BILL: Hey Shirley. What's the story on the party we're going to tonight? What time do we have to be there?

Shirley is sitting on the bed, ear to the phone, talking to one of her friends. She puts her hand over the mouthpiece and shouts.

SHIRLEY: It's a surprise party for Gilda at her girlfriend's house. They want everyone there by 9:00

BILL: Nine o'clock? My God it's twenty after eight already!

SHIRLEY: Don't worry. I'll be ready in a few minutes. I just have to take a quick shower and see what I feel like wearing.

Shirley turns back to the phone and continues her conversation. After a few minutes, Bill, growing more irritable, yells at her.

BILL: Cut the gab and get going!

Shirley excuses herself from the conversation and heads for the shower. Thirty minutes later she is putting the finishing touches to her makeup. Bill looks up from the newspaper he's been impatiently flipping through.

BILL: We'll never make it on time, Shirley.

SHIRLEY: I'll be ready in a minute, Bill. Look for the address. It's written on a paper napkin. It's on the kitchen table or in the bedroom on my night table, I think. Look in the kitchen first.

Bill is exasperated. He searches for the address without success.

BILL: I've looked in both places and can't find it. It's getting late!

SHIRLEY: Stop rushing me. I'll find it. I'm sure I put it in the kitchen, but if it's not there, maybe I left it in my white jacket, or in the car.

BILL: No wonder you can't find anything, Shirl. This place is always a mess and you're *always* late.

SHIRLEY: With everything I have to do around the house, I can't keep track of details. Here I am, almost dressed and planning to have a good time at a party, and you're nagging. You're spoiling the whole evening.

BILL: For God's sake, Shirley, what do you mean "details"? We're late for the party and you don't even know where you put the address. Where are we gonna go when we get in the car?

SHIRLEY: Stop fussing. I'll call Gloria, she'll know where it is. (Shirley dials quickly) Nuts, there's no answer. She's already left. She's the only one I know who's going to the party.

Bill, on his knees, is picking through some stray scraps of paper which have fallen under the table. The table itself is strewn with empty letter envelopes, half-read newspapers, magazines, coffee cup and saucer, and used paper napkins. Shirley is rummaging through the clutter. **SHIRLEY:** Here it is Bill! EXACTLY where I said it was!

A second skit involves Lori, who is waiting for her "auto-mechanic" husband to come home to dinner. Speaking to herself.

LORI: The roast has been ready since 7:00. It's 7:30 and Lew isn't home yet. I don't know what I'm going to do with that man. He never pays attention to time. I think I'll call the garage and see what's keeping him.

The door to the house slams and Lew enters.

LEW: Hello honey. I'm home.

LORI: I was about to call the garage. You're late, where were you?

LEW: Mrs. Kent is going away for the weekend. I had to finish her car.

LORI: I tried so hard to prepare a nice meal for you and now it's ruined. It's all dried out. You said you'd be home at 6:00, Lew.

LEW: It's all right, honey. I'm sure it will be fine. I'll be washed up in a minute.

LORI: I wish you would wash up at the garage before you come home. You know I like to keep the bathroom really clean. I just cleaned it today. It took me over an hour. You'll be in there two minutes and it'll be a mess.

LEW: Hey Lori, can't I relax in my own home? From the minute I come in all I hear is—"Don't get the sink dirty! Hang up your clothes! Hurry, up, the food is getting cold!"

LORI: (protests) All I'm trying to do is keep a clean and beautiful home and the minute I turn around you're messing it up.

Thank you, Sandy and Lou. It was a moving performance.

In the first sketch we clearly see the different styles that Bill (left-brain/neat) and Shirley (right-brain/sloppy) represent. We see Bill's

TURNING PLAY INTO WORK

concern with punctuality (time consciousness) and his exasperation with the disorder in the house (organization). Shirley is more into the experience of talking on the telephone (immediate gratification) and has not concerned herself with allowing enough time to shower, dress or even find the address of the party until the last moment (non-sequential thinking, timeless orientation).

In the second sketch the roles are reversed but the essential perceptual clash is evident.

At this point I'd like to shift gears again and go back to another one of the tests we designed to further clarify how we each experience the world differently.   See Illustration #3

Questionnaires depend on verbal definitions. They appeal to ideas and to language. Because there's a lot of room for error, in order to double-check our results, we designed another test based on nonverbal brain patterns called the Perceptual Differential Design Test. This test booklet which we have just distributed has paired designs. There is an A and B in every set. We want you to pick an ''A'' or ''B'' answer from the thirteen pair designs.

Say to yourself, ''Which one is more like me?'' Not ''Which one is prettier?'' But, ''Which one is more like me?'' You are to answer very quickly without giving your response a lot of thought. I am now handing out answer forms to use with the test booklet. Please wait until everyone has a copy before starting. See Illus. #4

READER STOP NOW

Take a few minutes to complete the following test. Use the enclosed worksheets, checking the column ''A'' and ''B'' to indicate your immediate preference. Take no more than five seconds to record your answers. Complete the test before reading further.

To score the PDDT, simply allow ten points for each ''A'' and ten points for each ''B'' answer. ''A'' are left-brain symbols; ''B'' are right-brain symbols. More ''B'' indicates right-brain dominance. More ''A'' indicates left-brain dominance.

To score the questionnaire taken earlier, consult the ''Questionnaire Answer Code'' on page (48). See whether your left or right brain answers are more predominant.

ODD COUPLE SYNDROME

 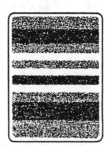 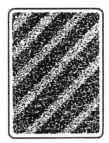

PERCEPTUAL DIFFERENTIAL DESIGN TEST

Illustration #3

A

B

WHICH DESIGN

IS MORE LIKE ME?

A

B

A   B

WHICH DESIGN

IS MORE LIKE ME?

A   B

b

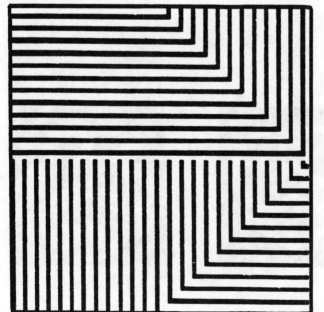

a

WHICH DESIGN IS MORE LIKE ME?

b

a

WHICH DESIGN IS MORE LIKE ME ?

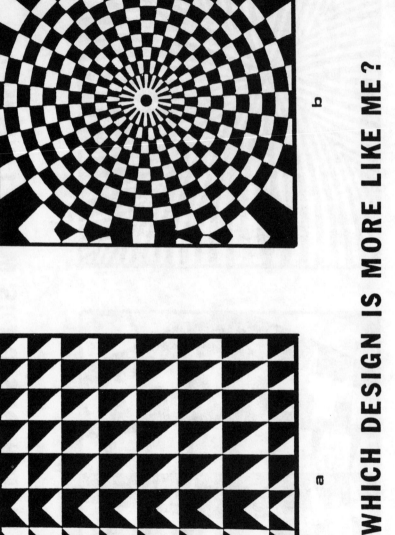

b

a

WHICH DESIGN IS MORE LIKE ME ?

B

A

WHICH DESIGN IS MORE LIKE ME?

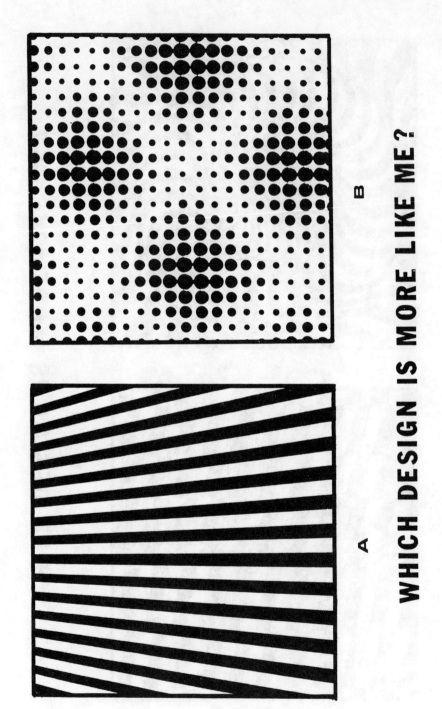

B

A

WHICH DESIGN IS MORE LIKE ME?

B

A

WHICH DESIGN IS MORE LIKE ME?

B

A

WHICH DESIGN IS MORE LIKE ME?

A

B

WHICH DESIGN IS MORE LIKE ME ?

B

A

WHICH DESIGN IS MORE LIKE ME?

Perceptual Differential Design Test
ANSWER FORM

* ANSWER QUICKLY.. TAKE 5 SECONDS OR LESS TO MAKE EACH CHOICE.
* ASK YOURSELF THE QUESTION BEFORE EACH NUMBERED SELECTION:

WHICH DESIGN IS MORE LIKE ME?

* THEN PUT A CHECK IN BOX A OR B.

RATE YOURSELF ON THE FOLLOWING SCALE

VERY NEAT O O O O O VERY SLOPPY
        1 2 3 4 5

NAME_____

MALE_____
FEMALE_____

Illustration #4

Perceptual Differential Design Test
ANSWER FORM

* ANSWER QUICKLY.. TAKE 5 SECONDS OR LESS TO MAKE EACH CHOICE.

* ASK YOURSELF THE QUESTION BEFORE EACH NUMBERED SELECTION:

WHICH DESIGN IS MORE LIKE ME?

* THEN PUT A CHECK IN BOX A OR B.

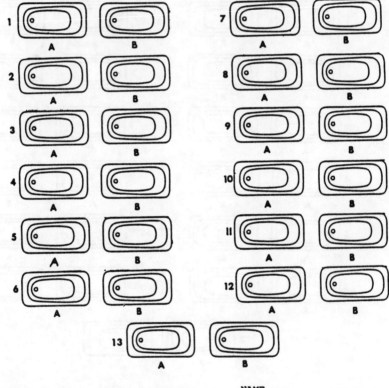

RATE YOURSELF ON THE FOLLOWING SCALE

VERY NEAT O O O O O VERY SLOPPY
          1 2 3 4 5

NAME_____

MALE_____
FEMALE

Perceptual Differential Design Test
ANSWER FORM

* ANSWER QUICKLY.. TAKE 5 SECONDS OR LESS TO MAKE EACH CHOICE.

* ASK YOURSELF THE QUESTION BEFORE EACH NUMBERED SELECTION:

WHICH DESIGN IS MORE LIKE ME?

* THEN PUT A CHECK IN BOX <u>A</u> OR <u>B</u>.

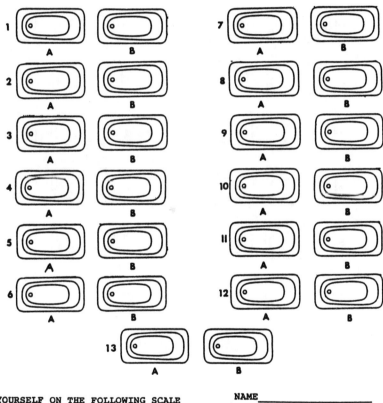

RATE YOURSELF ON THE FOLLOWING SCALE

VERY NEAT   O O O O O   VERY SLOPPY
           1 2 3 4 5

NAME_____

MALE_____
FEMALE

Perceptual Differential Design Test
ANSWER FORM

* ANSWER QUICKLY.. TAKE 5 SECONDS OR LESS TO MAKE EACH CHOICE.
* ASK YOURSELF THE QUESTION BEFORE EACH NUMBERED SELECTION:

WHICH DESIGN IS MORE LIKE ME?

* THEN PUT A CHECK IN BOX A OR B.

RATE YOURSELF ON THE FOLLOWING SCALE
VERY NEAT   O O O O O   VERY SLOPPY
            1 2 3 4 5

NAME_____

MALE_____
FEMALE

Perceptual Differential Design Test
ANSWER FORM

* ANSWER QUICKLY.. TAKE 5 SECONDS OR LESS TO MAKE EACH CHOICE.
* ASK YOURSELF THE QUESTION BEFORE EACH NUMBERED SELECTION:

WHICH DESIGN IS MORE LIKE ME?

* THEN PUT A CHECK IN BOX <u>A</u> OR <u>B</u>.

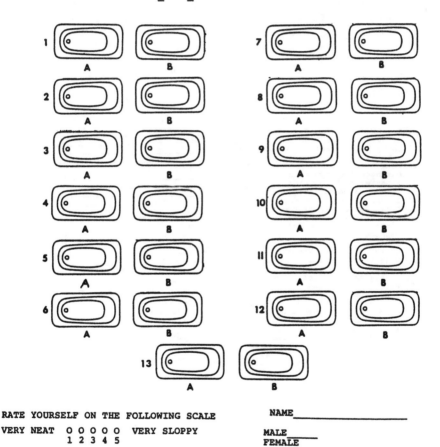

RATE YOURSELF ON THE FOLLOWING SCALE

VERY NEAT   O O O O O   VERY SLOPPY
           1 2 3 4 5

NAME_____

MALE____
FEMALE

ODD COUPLE SYNDROME ** QUESTIONNAIRE SCORING

ALWAYS & OFTEN ARE SCORED THE SAME
RARELY & NEVER ARE SCORED THE SAME
SOMETIMES HAS NO SCORE VALUE

L= LEFT BRAIN
R= RIGHT BRAIN
V= VISUAL
K= KINESTHETIC

NAME_____

	ALWAYS	OFTEN	SOMETIMES	RARELY	NEVER
1. I take good care of my possessions.	L	V			R
2. My decisions are more spontaneous than deliberate.	R				L
3. In my home I keep things well organized	L				R
4. I make concrete plans for the future	L				R
5. When I solve problems I take a playful rather than a business-like approach.	R				L
6. I pay my bills on time.	L				R
7. I tend to smoke, drink or eat too much.	R	K			L
8. I consider myself a saver rather than a thrower.	R				L
9. I am late for appointments.	R				L
10. I have trouble keeping my personal papers up to date.	R				L
11. I squeeze a tube of toothpaste from the bottom and replace the cap.	L	V			R
12. I am a careful craftsman.	L				R
13. I rely on my intuition in assessing new people	R	K			L
14. When I work on a project I plan things in detail.	L				R
15. I find keeping order a bother but do it promptly anyway.	L	V			R
16. I have trouble finding my keys.	R				L
17. When I start a task I follow through.	L				R
18. I consider myself self-disciplined.	L				R
19. I consider hunches very important in making decisions.	R	K			L
20. I am very concerned about my physical appearance.	L	V			R
21. On vacations, I enjoy spur-of-the-moment activities rather than set plans.	R				L
22. I am impelled to find specific places to put things.	L				R
23. I have a strong feeling to get up and move around when at a lecture or movie.	R	K			L
24. After planning my day I resist intrusions that would put me off track.	L				R

TOTAL..

TOTAL L/R ANSWERS =10 POINTS EACH
TOTAL V/K ANSWERS =10 POINTS EACH

LEFT_____
RIGHT_____
VISUAL_____
KINESTHETIC_____

Illustration #5

Compare the two tests to see if they point to the same brain dominance. In most cases the results agree. Occasionally a different of dominance is shown. This is usually due to influence of social condition on responses to the verbal questionnaire.

BACK TO THE WORKSHOP

Has everyone completed the test? You can now score your answer sheets. The right-brain symbols are "B" and the left-brain symbols are "A." What we want you to do is count up your "A"'s and "B"'s.

Bobbie, I'm guessing you had a lot of "A"'s and Valerie, you probably had a majority of "B"'s. Let me see your score sheets.

Bobbie, you're a left-brain type — very neat. You responded on this test with a great many left-brain symbols. So, how many "A"'s did you have?...Ten out of thirteen. And Valerie is a very right-brain type — sloppy — and how many "B"'s did you have?...Eleven! This is a perfect example. You know it wasn't set up. What did you have, Janet? "I had nine "A"'s." You had nine "A"'s. Okay. You're definitely a little more organized. You are the one who didn't want to be a "sloppy" today, remember!

The concept behind this test is that the left brain thinks in very structured, organized, straight-line symmetry, and the right brain thinks in terms of curvilinear lines, asymmetry, and movement. That's how the designs were constructed.

When making quick choices without thinking, without trying to work them out, 80% of the people who take this test respond just the way Bobbie and Valerie did. Also, we compare these tests to the questionnaires. The PDDT is a check on how a person responds to the questionnaire.

There is a great deal of conflict when neat and sloppy individuals live together, yet these differently oriented people are attracted to one another. When people are free to make choices, most people pick a person of the opposite type. Why do they do that? Why do people pick someone of the opposite type? It leads to a lot of conflict. Do people want conflict? Maybe they do! I think they don't, but invariably they end up in conflict when they're attracted to personality traits in another person which they feel lacking in themselves.

Ed, I overheard you talking about your partner who is sloppy and irritates you because you're very organized and very neat. However, he is very creative and has that ability to do things spontaneously. Somehow he manages to do things which are valuable for your business.

People who are very organized and left-brained, and people who are very casual and loose and creative have things to offer each other.

When you're attracted to someone, you think, "I don't really know what it is I love, but I love that person." Something that's mysterious, that's enticing about that person. And what it really is, is that we feel something lacking within ourselves. We're all aware unconsciously that we have certain ways of being in the world and we're also aware that we're lacking some of those things that we want. The left-brain person usually wants the kind of casual, easy, creative sense, and spontaneity they see in others.

They feel limited because everything they do has to be thought out. They have to think about it a hundred times; they have to worry about the consequences. After so much deliberation it often seems too late to do anything about it.

When they see another person who has that quality, they focus on it. "That person is very spontaneous...I'd like to be close to that; I'd like to have those things for myself." It's not verbalized that way, but that's the kind of attraction that occurs. The way the right-brain person sees the left-brain person is: "Phil is so responsible. He has everything under control; he knows how things are going to turn out and I feel comfortable when I'm with him."

The initial attraction that opposite types have for each other is valid. They're trying to complete that part of themselves which they feel is missing. But what happens? What happens a year later, two years later, four years later—when they're at each other's throats? "Why don't you pick your clothes up? You're so sloppy I can't stand it! You're always late for appointments! Every time we want to go someplace, I have to keep badgering you to get ready." And the sloppy person's always complaining: "You're so organized; you think everything out, there's no room for spontaneity. You can't enjoy anything. What's the matter with you?"

All of these complaints start to come up at a time when each person realizes that he can't have what the other person has, that the

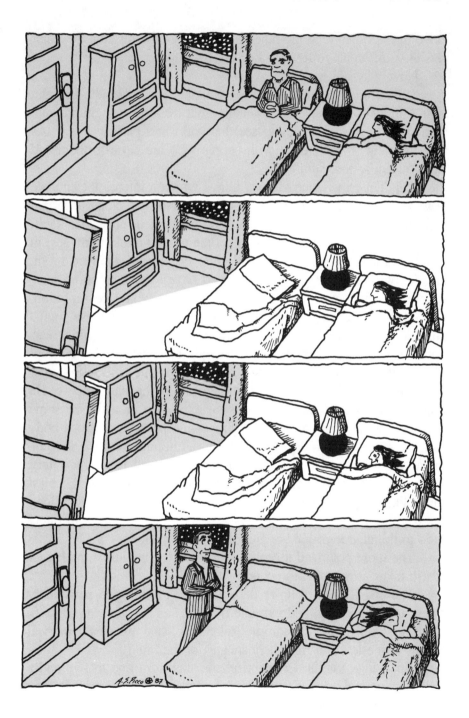

move from one style to the other is extremely difficult, that the other person is different from what they are by nature.

Now, why are we that way?

...Well, give or take...what we really believe is that left- or right-brain dominance is very much genetic, that from the day children are born, they have a tendency to see the world in a particular way. As they grow up, they interact with people who are close to them and are affected by the culture.

Children experience various things which reinforce their native way or conflict with it. As a result, a person develops a certain perceptual style. Left-brain people tend to think in concepts, ideas, words and thought, and right-brain people tend to think in images, in metaphors, in sensations. If a loud noise occurred in the next room, invariably, the right-brain person would have a body reaction in response to apparent danger. His initial reaction would be sensation. The left-brain person would say, "I wonder what that noise was?" His initial response would be idea, concept. Although the initial reaction would be body sensation for the right-brain person and concept for the left-brain person, each one would eventually shift to the other side. The left-brain person goes through an intellectual process. He might start thinking that there was an explosion or a fire or some disturbed person running amuck. This would be followed by a body reaction somewhat similar to that of the right-brain person. The right-brain person instinctively has a body reaction and looks for safety. The next reaction is thought about the possible cause for the blast much like the initial reaction of the left-brain person. But how long does it take to make the shift? Usually the time it takes is in direct ratio to the degree of left- or right-brain dominance.

The more polarized a person's left/right orientation is the longer it will take for the shift to occur.

The chart which follows depicts the left/right brain personality types in the moderate and extreme ranges. See Illustration #6

The Odd Couple Syndrome Relational Scale ascribes numerical values to the left and right hemispheres of the brain.

The range for the left hemisphere runs from one to five and a half, graduating from extreme left to moderate. The descriptive terms under the left hemisphere column refer to qualities which most left-brain people have. The person at point one would exhibit these qualities

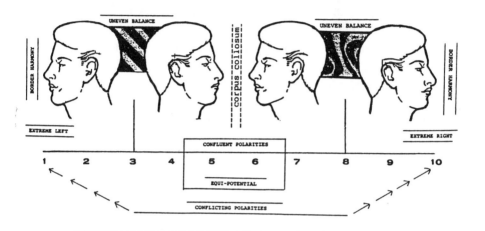

ODD COUPLE SYNDROME
RELATIONAL SCALE

LEFT HEMISPHERE

RIGHT HEMISPHERE

THE CHART ABOVE ILLUSTRATES THE DIFFERENT LEVELS OF
LEFT BRAIN/NEAT #1-5 AND RIGHT BRAIN/SLOPPY #6-10
PERCEPTUAL AWARENESS AND THE TYPES OF RELATIONSHIPS
THAT ARE CREATED BY THEIR COMBINATION.

LEFT HEMISPHERE	RIGHT HEMISPHERE
DELIBERATE	SPONTANEOUS
LOGICAL	INTUITIVE
CONTROLLED	EMOTIONAL
TREES	FOREST
LATER	NOW
NEAT	SLOPPY
VERTICAL	HORIZONTAL
PLAY INTO WORK	WORK INTO PLAY
OBSESSIVE	ADDICTIVE
IDEAS	SENSATION

Illustration #6

in the extreme. The person falling toward point five and a half would show the same qualities in moderation and he would also be more receptive to the qualities listed in the column under the right hemisphere.

The descriptive terms under the right hemisphere column are those most right-brain people have. Point ten represents the extreme, and five and a half the moderate. Again, five and a half right hemisphere would be receptive to qualities listed under left hemisphere.

The middle range on the scale from four and a half to six and a half represents the area of Equipotential or those people who are open to qualities of both sides.

On this chart (OCSRS), we mention several characteristics of left and right personality style. Each style arrives at behavior by a different thought process.

The left-brain person tends to postpone impulses until *later*. They ask themselves: "What is the consequence of what I do? I don't do it at this moment because if I do, this or that will happen, so I'll postpone it." Whereas, the right-brain person would say, "I must do it at this moment. I feel I want it right *now* and I'll do it right *now*."

Horizontal and *Vertical*—left-brain people seem to be vertical in thinking and in the way they operate with their material environment. Left-brain people are always hanging things up. They want everything in closets hanging up. Right brain people have everything on counters and floors. If there's a bed without someone lying on it, they will put something on it because it's handy. And they don't go out of their way to put things back in their customary place. Left and right brain people tend to be vertical and horizontal pretty much in their thinking and their behavior.

Left-brain people tend to turn *play into work*. If they're on vacation, they want to know what's going to happen within the next ten minutes. What are we doing tonight? Is it productive? What am I getting out of this vacation? They make a regular work schedule out of their play-time. Right-brain people tend to make *play out of work*. It is natural for the right-brain salesman to spend his time socializing and telling jokes. As a result he often falls behind schedule. His pattern is dictated by his brain orientation and is very difficult to change even if it endangers his job. Left-brained people are happiest when working and right-brained people are happiest when playing.

Larry and Scott are brothers, close in age but distant in perceptual style. Larry tested decidedly right-dominant and Scott was clearly left-oriented. Both of them are hard workers, but Larry would take periodic breaks during the day to kid around with his workmates while Scott would maintain a constant serious attitude toward his work. One afternoon Larry called Scott's office and as a joke told Scott's secretary that her boss Scott had just won the New York State Lottery. When Scott took the phone, he was indignant with Larry and told him to stop bothering him while he was at work.

According to a study conducted at a Chicago medical school, people with a "low pleasure capacity" make the best executives. The researchers who studied 88 executives said that people in that category are usually first in line for promotion. They conclude that "low pleasure seekers" concentrate on their work and don't allow "trivial" things like small talk and searing sunsets to distract them. Their fun-seeking colleagues on the other hand, tend to make less money and accept fewer responsibilities. They also complain more about work because they expect more free time and fewer deadlines.

Another important comparison between the left and right brain personality is the role played by obsessive and addictive traits.

The initial responses of left and right-brain people tend to be different. The left-brain person reacts with ideas and the right-brain person reacts with sensations.

The left-brain person, the "obsessive," tries to organize his life to the smallest details, avoid unpredictable situations by planning ahead rather than leaving things to the last minute, and is very involved with ideas and thoughts. If a left-brain person has psychological problems, that person will reflect the "obsessive/compulsive" personality.

Right brain persons tend to be addictive because they respond so strongly to sensation. Activities like eating, smoking, drinking, gambling, and taking drugs are not thought out. People who are addictive do not think about their behavior but act on impulse to satisfy the sensations of their bodies. It is the primacy of the right brain's sensation experiences which makes them particularly susceptible to addictive behavior. When right-brain people have psychological problems, they are generally related to the Hysterical Personality (impulsivity, dependency, excessive emotionality).

LEFT/RIGHT RELATIONSHIP STYLES

There are four types of relationships which grow out of left/right personality factors.

Uneven Balance

The term "uneven balance" refers to two Neats or two Sloppies living together whose left/right brain perceptual style is the same.

In the case of two Neats, they are both in the range of 1-5½. Sloppies fall in the range of 5½-10 on the Odd Couple Relationship Scale.

The left-brain oriented people are motivated toward organization and appearance. The right-brains are not motivated toward organization and appearance, but toward postponement of chores and allowing things to be loose.

In both types of the Uneven Balance usually one party considers himself neater than the other, and will accept all the major responsibility for keeping things in order (basic housekeeping: cooking, cleaning, shopping, paying bills, etc.)

In each situation the neater party is critical of the lesser neat person. This criticism can be the surface manifestation of deeper issues reflective of a struggle for power in the relationship.

Conflicting Polarities

The conflicting polarity relationships are marked by constant strife and clash over Neat/Sloppy issues. These people are represented on the *OCSRS* by the extreme left 1 and 2 and the extreme right 9 and 10. This is the classic Felix/Oscar relationship which relates directly to the dichotomy between left and right hemisphere perceptual style. However, they represent no more than 20% of the people we have studied in our Odd Couple project.

Their behavior, to some degree, is an exaggerated example of how the other 80% acts. The extreme 1 and 2 and the extreme 9 and 10 closely reflect all the left and right cognitive perceptions listed respectively on the Odd Couple Syndrome Relationship Scale.

Conflicting Polarity not only describes a relationship between two different people, but often the split within a single person. A person with conflicting polarity experiences both extremes at different times but seldom integrates the two. This person at times may be very neat, obsessive, analytical and very time-conscious—like the left-brain person, and at other times—like the right-brain person, he may be irresponsible about time, very sloppy, addictive and illogical.

An example might be the bachelor who comes home from work, drops his clothes on door knobs and counters, throws the mail on a pile of unopened letters—but keeps his closets and dresser drawers in perfect order.

Converging Polarities

The term Converging Polarities is used to describe those people who fall in the middle range of the scale, that is, 4 to 7. For example, a left-brain 4, and a right-brain 7 understand each other because they are not at opposite extremes. These relationships are most productive, exciting and growth-oriented. Each person is more open to the different style of the other person.

When applied to the individual we call it "equipotential." Persons who fall between 4 and 7 on the scale have the ability to move back and forth smoothly between the left and right hemisphere, integrating the qualities of both, and more readily calling upon left-brain logic and right-brain intuition at the appropriate moment.

Border Harmony

Border Harmony relationships consist of people represented on the scale by 1 and 2 and 9 and 10, sharing the borders with their own type and achieving relatively happy relationships. The left 1 and 2 types value security and predictability while living without risk and excitement. The right 9 and 10 value risk and excitement while usually sacrificing security and predictability. Both of these kinds of relationships are characterized by mutual acceptance and differ from the Uneven Balance group by the absence of a power struggle. *Acceptance and cooperation* is substituted for *control and competition*.

Now we can return to those unanswered queries concerning relationships in the light of the "Odd Couple Syndrome." We believe all relationships can be improved but within limits, and that the way

in which we approach the other person and the feelings and attitudes we have about him have a lot to do with how much change can occur. We have a system called the *Three A's:*
ACCEPTANCE...APPRECIATION...ACCOMMODATION.

ACCEPTANCE of the fact that the other person ''is'' who he is. Although that person's behavior is at times irritating, it is not motivated by a desire to make your life miserable.

We can *APPRECIATE* those qualities in the other person that we do not have. (Remember—that is what inspired the initial attraction. You have to bring yourself back to that *APPRECIATION.*)

Now, if you have the *acceptance* and the *appreciation*, you have the ground for *ACCOMMODATION*. Your husband keeps telling you: ''Vivian, get the stuff off the doorknobs; don't lay things on the counters—you know it makes me uncomfortable when the place looks this way.'' You can consider: Well, I understand how he feels about it; it upsets him if things are like that, so I will *accommodate*. I can make those changes. On the other hand, if you have the habit of being somewhat late in getting ready for a date, your husband might accommodate by being patient. There are a variety of issues when accommodation might apply, but ACCOMMODATIONS are only available when both people ACCEPT and APPRECIATE each other.

Almost everyone carries some stress home from their day's work. When a right-brain person is in a job that demands left-brain qualities (logical, rational, detailed-oriented skills) there is additional stress which is not ordinarily recognized. Left-brain jobs like bookkeeping and engineering fall into this category. When right-brain people who hold these kinds of jobs come home, there is a tendency for them to become more extreme in their customary habits. Their sloppiness is intensified.

There are left-brain people who work as artists and in the theatre where right-brain qualities are required who also have this additional stress. When they get home, their tendency is to increase their longing for neatness and order.

If you're living with a person who has a job requiring qualities in conflict with their natural style, we suggest you try to be aware of the extra stress that person is under. Calling upon the three ''A''s (Acceptance, Appreciation, Accommodation) at this time is more dif-

READER STOP NOW !

WORKLIFE ACTIVITIES CHECK LIST

UNDERLINE ALL THE WORDS THAT DESCRIBE WHAT YOU DO IN AN AVERAGE WEEK

LIST 1

accounting	directing	policymaking
administering	dissecting	prioritizing
advocating	editing	purchasing
allocating	enforcing	reading
analyzing	examining	reasoning
assigning	expediting	recommending
bookkeeping	explaining	reconciling
budgeting	filing	recording
calculating	guiding	reporting
clarifying	identifying	reproducing
classifying	implementing	reviewing
collecting	initiating	scheduling
compiling	judging	screening
computing	leading	self-motivating
contracting	managing	summarizing
controlling	memorizing	supervising
copying	modifying	systematizing
critiquing	motivating	tabulating
deciding	ordering	updating
defining	organizing	validating

TOTAL LIST 1_____

LIST 2

adapting	demonstrating	negotiating
addressing	discovering	nurturing
assembling	drafting	observing
assisting	drawing	operating
building	enlisting	painting
caring	exercising	performing
catering	farming	preparing
climbing	feeding	processing
composing	fixing	proposing
counseling	gathering	reacting
counting	humoring	reflecting
creating	innovating	relating
dancing	installing	repairing
decorating	manipulating	restoring
delivering	mapping	scanning
servicing	styling	translating
shaping	supporting	troubleshooting
simplifying	surveying	typing
singing	symbolizing	visualizing
staging	tending	wishing

TOTAL LIST 2_____

adapted from Whole Brain Thinking/Wonder & Donovan 1984

Illustration #7

ficult because of your own reactiveness to their irritibility, but it also is more necessary if you wish to avoid needless conflict.

The chart on the previous page (*Illustration #7* will help you determine whether the general activities that fill your workday are predominantly left- or right-brain.

Underline all the words which comprise the things you are likely to do in an average week. Count all the underlined activities in Group #1 and Group #2.

Group #1 consists of left-brain tasks and Group #2 consists of right-brain ones. The list with the highest number will indicate if your worklife favors left- or right-hemisphere skills.

It is important to be aware of how your own perceptual style relates to the demands of your daily activity. If the requirements of your work match your natural style, your job will feel more comfortable. If there is disparity between them, increased stress will be experienced. Where there is a contrast between work and style, awareness is the key to reducing stress. Then the options are clear: You can change the type of work you do or modify the things you do on that job by delegating some tasks to others. A right-brain person in a left-brain job can minimize stress by the use of organizing aids and devices (files, printed forms, etc.) A left-brain person in a right-brain occupation who feels under stress must experience the satisfaction of completion. So digging in and finishing a task will reduce the stress. In both cases, attending to the stress by finding ten minutes to relax or meditate at the point of discomfort is a very helpful response.

Jacquelyn Wonder, a management consultant who conducts seminars for corporations, uses the left/right brain model in her training sessions. She describes the left side as the home of discipline and organization and the right side as the home of intuition and inspiration. In her book, *Whole Brain Thinking*, Ms. Wonder suggests many useful techniques for brain balancing and stress. She recommends the voluntary blocking of the left or right side of the brain in order to more fully access the other side.

In order to switch from left to right, you might use "mental suspenders" which over- or under-stimulate the left brain. Mental suspenders evade the left brain and access the right in two ways: by overloading the left with details, or by starving the left for information until it falls into boredom. Deprivation of sensory stimulation, an overload of words or demands for concentration, exhausts the left and allows a right-brain takeover. Instrumental music, rhythm, flashing lights, repetition sounds, a warm bath and gentle massage also contribute to switching into your right brain.

Ms. Wonder sees switching to the left brain as a form of focused concentration. When studying for a long period of time, there is a tendency to space out. She suggests that one should pause at the end of each concept and rephrase it in your mind. Another technique is to establish a cue that will remind you to refocus.

It can be tugging at your earlobe, drawing a circle on your note pad or taking a deep breath.

As a left-brain training, she suggests keeping records of everything: Your household belongings, car mileage and investments. Watch the clock, the stock and baseball scores. She believes that simply heightening your awareness of time, numbers and money will increase your comfort with matters of the left brain.

Although we believe that the basic tendency of most people is to favor their dominant side, it is also possible to approach more balance by conscious awareness and the use of special exercises.

At this point the workshop was opened up to questions from the audience.

Someone from the audience would like to know whether persons of opposite extremes can have fulfilling relationships.

I've known of some couples that were extreme and got along very well because they really respected all those differences in the other person. However, they had to fulfill a lot of their own needs. They didn't enjoy the same things. A right-brain person might enjoy walking in a forest, going to art galleries, etc. A very left-brain person might say, "You know, you've seen one forest, you've seen them all! You've seen one art gallery, you've seen them all!" There may be many things those people won't do together, but if there is enough unity and love and respect between them, they can make a go of it, as long as they don't try to change the other person..

One of the workshop members asks: "What if a parent's brain dominance differs from her child's?"

The auditory messages that we get as children can be very powerful and can conflict with our left- or right-brain orientation. A common example is the left-brain mother who is constantly telling her right-brain child such things as "You *shouldn't* feel that way." "Everything should be very neat." "You're not paying attention to the way your room looks." At such times, the right-brain child is involved in images and metaphors and seeing the world in a particular way. The mother's auditory messages tend to be upsetting.

The child may respond in a very conformist way to please the parent, or might rebel. Rebellion is not an easy road to take, but it is often chosen when the child's way of being is violated. It brings on anger at the parent and a desire to retaliate. Sloppiness is a typical way for a child to upset the parent. It is important to know that this form of rebellion often serves as a pressure relief valve where parent/child brain differences are a factor.

Judy asked, if adolescents have set left/right brain styles. We are not able to see a set pattern in adolescents. In general adolescence is a particularly difficult stage of life. All adolescents go through many extreme changes both chemical and physical. Some may be consistently very neat and organized, others very sloppy and disorganized. Some will continually shift from one style to the other.

Another question asked was, "How do I become more left-brain"?

Changing brain dominance is very difficult and seldom necessary. Every right-brain person has left-brain capabilities. Each situation has to be viewed as a specific problem to be solved. I recently met a young woman who was six months into her first experience as an elementary school teacher. She was an extreme right-brain type. She told me about the initial difficulties she encountered in her work. She was so disorganized that she never knew where to find the crayons or paper required to run the class. After one month of confusion, she arranged to come in early every morning for a full week. The time was used to organize her closets and desk and box things properly. She actually drew up a chart showing where each thing was to be kept. After that week she no longer spent her energy wastefully and instead was able to direct her efforts toward imagination, inventiveness and enthusiasm to the advantages of the children. In other words, by gearing to a specific situation and facing her so-called "deficiency," she was able to solve the problem by calling on her left-brain capacities. A left brain teacher would have automatically organized her closets and avoided the confusion.

Toward More Balance

This is a good place for us to introduce what we call a brain-balancing exercise which is designed to help us get the sense of integrating the two sides of our brain.

(Readers: get some colored crayons and use the two blank pages which follow to participate in the exercises.)

First, we are going to give each one of you two pieces of drawing paper and you're going to draw a picture. We have some crayons here. You're going to have a little fun now. (Everybody takes the colors of their choice.)

Now draw a picture of your favorite thing: it might be a house; it might be a person; it could be a dog; it could be flowers, a tree; it could be a landscape—whatever you want. The picture should be something you like to draw...You do not have to be an artist to do this. Everyone has adequate ability to succeed at this. Please start...

Now that everyone has completed their drawing, stand up, close your eyes and we're going to put on some music. Feel the music. (Beethoven Piano Concerto) Now! Raise your right arm slowly in front of you and experience the music with your arm as though you are conducting the orchestra. Be aware your left brain is controlling the right side of your body. Experience the music going all the way down into the right side of your body. (Exercise is done very slowly to the music for about two minutes.) Now the exercise consists of using the left arm to conduct the orchestra for two minutes experiencing the right brain controlling the left side of the body. Now very, very slowly, open your eyes and sit down, turn the paper over to the other side of the drawing you have just completed (at home, use page 2). Draw the same picture again. See if you can keep the same feeling that you experienced when you were listening to the music and do this drawing once more.

Now, compare the picture that you've just done and see if there is any difference between the first and second drawing.

Each person compared the two pictures while I walked around to observe the differences which had occurred.

Yes! There is a real improvement. That's what usually happens. We've done this exercise with hundreds of people. They usually experi-

DRAWING 1

DRAWING   2

ence a definite shift. Sometimes we do this exercise in pairs where neats and sloppies who had paired up originally will do the same picture so that the left-brain person will make one line and the right-brain person will make another line. They'll create a picture together. The picture is very full of conflict. You can see where all the straight and linear lines were made by the neat person and all the curvilinear lines were made by the sloppy person. Following the exercise, when a second picture was done jointly, it was much more harmonious, much more flowing. In almost all cases, changes between the first and second pictures were very dramatic. As you can see, the pictures done here today demonstrate the shift which takes place.

Dotty, Let me see your pictures. That's a dramatic difference — the first one is rather stiff and empty. In the second one, the house is more colorful and looks lived-in. There is smoke coming from the chimney and the garden looks lush.

The reader who has done the exercise at home will clearly see the changes when comparing the two drawings.

By increasing the awareness of your body/mind connection through this exercise, you are actually improving the balance between your left and right brain. Many people who have used this method have reported improved problem-solving skills.

We encourage you to do this exercise on your own. Put the music on, move your right arm, visualize your left brain controlling the right side and vice versa. You will be giving your whole body an integrated feeling. You bring to your consciousness a process which you usually do automatically.

I'd like to point out how different activities call more heavily on one side of the brain or the other. For example, let us consider two different kinds of music. Classical music is very structured, organized, rational and logical. When classical music is rehearsed, the same notes and agreed timing are repeated until the conductor is satisfied.

Jazz music is quite different. Traditionally, jazz is not written. It is a right-brain music which is expressed differently every time it is played. In most cases, the jazz musician does not plan his performance but plays from some inner expression. Unlike the classical music, jazz is almost pure right-brain activity.

Making love, like jazz, is almost purely a right-brain activity. Brain surgery is best performed when the surgeon is in his left brain.

These examples show how different activities make greater demands on the left or right side of the brain. Both classical and jazz music are artistic expressions. The point we'd like to make is that the left brain is not insensitive and nonartistic and the right brain is not the repository of all creativeness.

In answer to a question from the audience.

Yes, there are some ways in which psychology and our developmental history are more important than the perceptual factor. For example, I have a friend who has a twenty-three-year-old daughter and when she lived at home, her room was an absolute mess. Her mother went crazy trying to keep her room in order. Her clothes were always lying all over the place. Three years ago, she got her own apartment in Manhattan and it was kept absolutely immaculate. When her mother came to visit, she said: "Judy, I can't believe it! This is your place? You did this yourself? That's wonderful!"

My friend told me that Judy came home a couple of weeks ago to spend a weekend there, and when it was all over, her room was a mess! The mother said: "Judy, how can you do that? I saw your apartment a couple of weeks ago and it was so neat?" Judy responded: "Mom, something happens when I come into this house. I just don't understand it." Obviously, Judy wanted to feel like a little girl again; her psychological need dominated. Her behavior was not guided by her usual left/right perception. Her perception was overridden by her psychological drive to re-experience herself as a child. There are many psychological factors that have an impact on our neat/sloppy behavior.

We are about to close the meeting so I would like to present an exercise. Please push your chairs toward the back of the room. Form a circle. Hold the hand of the person you did the opening exercise with so that we have alternating neats and sloppies. Then drop your hand and turn to the right, making a complete circle, each one facing the back of an opposite type. Each person, put your hands on the person's shoulders who is in front of you and massage that person's back. (Odd Couple Theme is playing on tape.)

This exercise integrated the left and right energies in the group and was experienced as relaxing and pleasant.

End of edited transcript of workshop at New York State Counselor Convention

Chapter 3
Differences In Left/Right Brain Process

We have discovered through research, workshops, questionnaires and various experiments that the Odd Couple Syndrome theory is a tool for understanding both our interpersonal and intrapersonal relationships. Neat/Sloppy behavior affords us a window into the brain through which we can trace a network of personality traits; linking neatness with left-hemisphere dominance and sloppiness with right-hemisphere dominance increase understanding of our behavior. Each side of our brain perceives and experiences reality in a unique way, thus affecting the way we view ourselves and others.

As we stressed earlier, no person is exclusively 'right brain' or 'left brain.' Only a small percentage of individuals inhabit the extreme.

Most of us choose to employ a particular brain hemisphere in response to the demands of a specific task. The measure of which side is dominant depends on the frequency of brain side use. In many cases the choice of hemisphere is exclusive rather than balanced, that is, only one hemisphere is employed for the task, whereas the use of both would be better. As a matter of fact, we would be unable to effectively complete a task very well without calling on both sides.

Left- and right-hemisphere thinking are composed of two different kinds of mental processes often viewed as opposed to one another or as mutually antagonistic. Actually, left and right cognition are, more often than not, complementary and mutually reinforcing.

The right hemisphere operates predominantly through nonverbal thought-forms (images, metaphors), arranging and rearranging them, combining them and creating new ones from combinations of old and new experiences. The right brain usually operates below the range of consciousness: we are aware of the results but not the process. The left hemisphere formalizes our ideas, translates them into concrete verbal terms, and produces and verifies whatever reasoning chains are necessary to support them. It operates primarily through words, numbers and other concrete thought-forms, predominantly within the range of consciousness; where we are aware of the process.

Brain researchers are as yet unclear as to why many of us choose one side more than the other, or why we don't, as part of natural process, alternate regularly between them as each task demands. Whether the reason is genetic, psychological, developmental, habitual or all of the above, researchers agree that every experience can be enhanced by the integration of both hemispheres, and that more scientific information and exploration are necessary to better understand the process.

In any case, left/right brain dominance exists and profoundly affects human behavior. We have observed that each hemisphere gives rise to its own sequence of cognitive expression: When the right brain is dominant, the sequence is *feeling, action, thought*. When the left brain is dominant, the sequence is reversed, that is, *thought, action, feeling*. These patterns clearly parallel the Neat/Sloppy issue, as well as such diverse activities as shopping, eating and problem solving.

For example, the right/brain dominant, after using a household tool, will drop it where it was last used:

Feeling and Action: Having accomplished the task or having been frustrated by difficulty, the right-brain dominant loses interest in using the tool and so disposes of it indiscriminantly (a form of immediate gratification.)

Thought: Thought seldom emerges at all in these cases until the right brain dominant again needs the tool.

If the left-brain dominant used the same tool, the sequence would probably be thought, action, feeling.

Thought and Action: Having repaired, reinforced or installed some item with the help of this tool, the left-brain dominant would clean up the site and return the tool to its original and proper storage place. The thinking behind this action is that, taking the time to put the tool away will save time in the future (time conscious).

The Feeling: After the tool is returned, the left-brain dominant feels relieved and satisfied that order has been restored.

The following account related by a woman at a workshop further illustrates the presence of these sequences in the left and right brain, respectively.

It was during my lecture on the sequence of cognitive expression (feeling, action, thought vs. thought, action, feeling) that she realized the incident she was about to tell reflected her Odd Couple relationship with her husband.

The essence of her story is as follows: She and her husband were shopping for a gift. They had decided to buy their friend a belt for his birthday. The friend was a large man requiring a size 44 belt which was not easy to find. The couple went from store to store at a shopping mall, going directly to the belt display in each shop. The wife recalled how they argued about the different ways to approach the quest. Her husband, a left-brain dominant, would promptly examine the belt sizes at the top of the rack for a size 44. If he didn't find one, he would be inclined to hurry his wife out of the store. (Initial expression: thought followed by action.)

On the other hand, the woman, a right-brain dominant, upon encountering each rack, was fascinated by the variety of styles and colors. She was more concerned with which belts appealed to her asthetically than with the belt sizes. She would examine every belt that interested her and was angered by her husband's impatience. (Initial expression: feeling followed by action.) In the course of arguing, he would say, ''What difference does it make if you like the belt or not if they don't have the right size?'' And she would say, ''What difference does it make if they have the right size if you don't like the belt?'' As the woman told the story and understood the difference in the process between herself and her husband, she laughed.

It is our impression that when left-brain dominant and right-brain dominant couples attend a theatre or dance performance, the initial perceptual experience for both is different. The left-brain dominant will focus on the themes, ideas, structure and sequential patterns, whereas the right-brain dominant will be moved by the color, movement, emotional interactions and immediate impact of the performance. Obviously, both of these approaches are important and the degree to which each person can move from his/her initial responses toward the opposite hemisphere will determine how much he or she can enjoy the experience.

In considering the interaction between an Odd Couple, the initial responses to most situations for the left-brain dominants will be symbolic, idea- and concept-oriented, while the initial responses of the right-brain dominants will be sensorial and emotional. We find that considerable integration is possible between them when awareness, openness and acceptance are exercised. Consider the following analysis of these qualities:

AWARENESS: To be conscious of the habitual pattern of your own response. Thought/action/feeling or feeling/action/thought.

OPENNESS: To be open to the habitual response pattern opposite to that of your own. And to face the slow, hard task of integration.

ACCEPTANCE: To see both styles of response as valid and acceptable.

Chapter 4
Harmony and Discord
in The Odd Couple Relationship

Living with a person of the opposite type will, at times, lead to upsets, irritations and arguments. These clashes can become endless episodes wherein each person is trying to prove his point or present opportunities to develop new strategies for harmony.

We believe the three A's — ACCEPTANCE, APPRECIATION and ACCOMMODATION, along with some basic communication guides, can be useful in developing a harmonious relationship. The personal account that follows will demonstrate the value of this approach:

Max and I have been friends for over thirty years. For fifteen years, he has lived on the West Coast and I have lived in New York. During these years we managed to share our lives through letters, phone calls and visits.

Both psychotherapists, we have been particularly aware of how often Neat/Sloppy complaints come up in discussion. We have seen many who share common values and strong feelings for one another get caught up in conflicts over what appear to be trivial issues.

Gradually, through discussion of this apparent paradox, we became aware of our own differences. One of us kept his desk neat and organized, which, in turn, reflected the general state of the room. The other had a desk cluttered with papers, books and assorted bric-a-brac extending out to the four corners of the room.

Our differences were always a source of banter and laughter. The laughter was always followed by a "Thank God we don't live together!"

During the spring of 1980, Max rented his house in California and established a temporary residence in New York in order to work on a program designed for autistic children. We were then developing the theory of the "Odd Couple Syndrome" and it occurred to me that it might be a good idea to use Max's visit as a live-in laboratory for our studies.

When I proposed the experiment, he responded, "It sounds like an exotic form of masochism: My living with a Felix is not the kind of torture I particularly relish. My sloppy ways will drive you to distraction and probably turn old friends into new enemies. There must be a more humane way." It was all finally settled. We would live together.

There we were, two divorced men who had lived alone for years, now living together. We both were established psychotherapists who enjoyed our work and were generally happy with our individual lifestyles. I lived in an orderly, artfully decorated apartment. I am a photographer. I enjoy music, reading, and quiet. I am also a gourmet cook whose diet includes whole grains and mineral water. Max's home in California is comfortable and very casual. He furnished his New York apartment with barely any attention to aesthetics. He is gregarious and outgoing, likes spectator sports, eats junk food and loves beer.

Our styles of everyday living were clearly at opposite ends of the "Odd Couple" syndrome. But I was convinced that our cohabitation could be productive in furthering our study.

On Max's birthday (November 19th) he pulled up to my apartment in his rusty, 1967 Ford Mustang. I came out to greet him and help unload his car. The backseat was littered with clothes and overstuffed suitcases. Desk supplies wrapped in rubber bands and food from his refrigerator were piled into plastic shopping bags.

When I reached for a suitcase it opened. Clothes, books, shaving equipment, a baseball mit and a back scratcher made from two plastic forks taped together all tumbled onto the sidewalk. The sublime mess gave me a sinking sensation in the pit of my stomach.

Max, unruffled, casually stuffed everything back into the suitcase and carried it up the steps. When I walked into the apartment, I noticed that he had distributed his belongings on my Danish walnut dining room table, my two matching chairs and the floor. I panicked, quickly whisking the suitcases off the table.

"That's a hand-polished finish on that table! It scratches very easily."

"I'm sorry. I didn't realize I might damage it."

"It's common sense. You don't put a heavy suitcase on top of a dining room table."

"If I had common sense, I wouldn't be here in the first place."

"Don't be sarcastic. I hope you're going to be more careful, because I don't want any of my furnishings ruined."

Suddenly my friend burst into laughter: "Do you see what's going on? This is the very stuff we're supposed to be studying." Before he had finished talking, I was laughing too. Subsequently, we dumped Max's stuff into the guest bedroom and we went out to celebrate his birthday.

In the months that followed, it was our constant observation of the other's unique way of doing things that helped us understand the intricacies of left/right-brain functioning. We couldn't ask for better subjects: He and I epitomized the classic Neat/Sloppy polarity. On our own questionnaires, Max scored high as a right-brain/kinesthetic sloppy. I was clearly a left-brain/visual neat. We noted that almost every aspect of our personal behavior reflected our own individual style.

One afternoon, during lunch, we fell into a heated discussion about some aspect of the Odd Couple theory. As we were talking, I watched the crust from Max's sandwich crumble over the table as he ate. It annoyed me to no end, so without missing a beat, I lifted his elbow and swept the bread crumbs (which were about to fall onto the floor) toward the center of the table. A flash of recognition passed between us: We laughted and continued our discourse.

All of the typical Neat/Sloppy issues became issues for us, including toothpaste-squeezing, clothes hanging, accumulating vs throwing-away preferences and disagreements over time-consciousness. It was primarily through observing our perceptual clashes in light of the Odd Couple theory that we developed the three A's: ACCEPTANCE, APPRECIATION, ACCOMMODATION.

During the course of our living together, we noted that despite our many differences we got along quite well. We wondered why this was so. We reviewed our feelings and behavior toward each other and realized that:

1. We did not have the need to change one another. There was *acceptance* of each as we were.
2. We found that our different orientations complemented one another and taught us how to deal better with those who are different from ourselves. We had deep *appreciation* of the other's unique qualities.
3. With the absence of control and the benefits of the differences, we were inclined to *accommodate* the other's requests.

During Max's sojourn, we had countless incidents of Neat/Sloppy conflicts, many ending with irritation, frustration and hurt feelings.

On one occasion, I had returned from a weekend away to find that Max had used my private bathroom rather than his own and had managed to rearrange the position of every toilet item on the counter. He also left his toothpaste and brush dangling from one of the ceramic glass holders. He was not inclined to replace the toilet paper and draped wet towels over the door knob across the window sill and toilet tank.

The three A's not withstanding, I lashed out at him:

"You incurable slob. What did you do to my bathroom?" He responded apologetically: "Oh! Sorry about that. I was going to straighten it up before you got home. The plumber won't be able to fix the sink in my bathroom before Monday."

"You still didn't have to leave my bathroom looking like a pigsty."

Then he attacked me for being an obsessive neatnik. The incident ended in anger, with hurt feelings on both sides.

A few days later we could examine the confrontation with some detachment and ask ourselves what went wrong and how we might have handled the situation more productively.

We realized that there were strong feelings evoked within us. Instead of expressing them honestly, we attacked each other. This is one of the cardinal symptoms of bad communication which we as professional therapists are always quick to recognize in our patients. There we were falling into the same trap.

It was essential not only to focus on the three A's as an aid to understanding our differences, but to observe all the classical rules of effective interpersonal communication:

1. Describe what is bothering you.
2. Express how you feel, and
3. Focus on solutions, not blame.

(1) DESCRIBE WHAT IS BOTHERING YOU: What was bothering me was not that Max used my bathroom or that he had a different sense of order than I did, but that my bathroom was disorganized 'by my standards,' and that it would take me time to get it back to the way I wanted it.

(2) EXPRESS HOW YOU FEEL: I was feeling upset and disoriented. I was angry that someone would use my private bathroom and leave it in such disarray.

(3) FOCUS ON SOLUTIONS, NOT BLAME: In other words, productive communication technique and the three A's.

If I had been able to say to Max at the time, "When I walked into my bathroom, I was shocked and upset to see what a mess it was. I organize my things in a personal way, so that they are accessible to me. When someone changes the arrangement of things in my private space, it upsets me," I would have spared us both some hurt feelings.

Expressing the problem paves the way for mutually agreeable solutions. Surely Max had no intention of causing me the upset. His perception of order was clearly different from mine. In our subsequent discussion, the use of the three A's helped us arrive at a mutual understanding. If our communication initially had been more effective, we would have avoided the unnecessary blaming, which serves only to postpone solutions, if not make them impossible.

It was indeed our three A's prescription that made our experiment at first only bearable, but eventually productive and rewarding.

Chapter 5
Testing

To substantiate the theory that left/right brain function determines Neat/Sloppy behavior, we developed a test instrument (semantic differential response test) which would reveal the subject's primary brain organization and its correlation to Neatness and Sloppiness.

The response test, or questionnaire, consisted of twenty-four true-or-false questions. Five hundred of these were distributed. At the end of the test the subject rates himself on a scale from #1 (very neat) to #5 (very sloppy). Twelve of the twenty-four questions were left-brain oriented, twelve were right-brain oriented. If the subject rates himself one or two on the self-appraisal neat-to-sloppy scale, our prediction was that he would answer "True" to a majority of left-brain questions. Likewise, should the subject rate himself four or five, he would have answered "True" to a majority of right-brain questions.

The results from the testing were encouraging but imprecise. The test itself needed revisions, so we reworked and circulated two more series of questionnaires before we were satisfied with its design. We changed words, rephrased sentences and changed questions until we were reasonably sure that what we included would be understood clearly by the respondents. We substituted the choice of *True* or *False* with the more flexible, *Always, Often, Sometimes, Rarely* or *Never* thereby offering a wider range of response.

The new questionnaire consisted of twenty-four statements relating to left/right-brain-visual/kinesthetic mental processing.

The twelve left-brain statements we presumed would be answered *Always* or *Often* by a neat person. For example, Question #3 reads: "In my home I keep things well organized." This is a characteristic function of the left hemisphere, that is, sorting, filing, organization for future use.

The twelve right-brain statements would most likely be answered *Always* or *Often* by a sloppy person. Consider for example Question #21: "On vacations, I enjoy spur-of-the-moment activities rather than set plans." The right hemisphere, more comfortable with spontaneity, spurns organized arrangements.

Four of the twelve left-brain statements are also visual dominant statements. #20: "I am very concerned about my physical appearance." The left brain is outer-directed, concerned about others' impressions of them. The visual dominance intensifies this concern.

Four of the twelve right-brain statements are also kinesthetic statements. #19: "I consider hunches very important in making decisions." The right-brain process employs a non-sequential pattern association to understanding a problem. The 'hunch' is the link connecting these separate thoughts, making synthesis possible. The 'hunch' has a sensorial, kinesthetic quality to it.

Scoring the Questions

Each of the 24 questions = 10 points.

The respondent who rates himself a #1 or #2 (neat) should answer left-brain questions "always" or "often," and right-brain questions "rarely" or "never," at least 15 times for a score of 150. A respondent who rates himself #4 or #5 (sloppy) should score similarly on the opposite scale.

The four visual/left-brain and kinesthetic/right brain statements are not always favored by left-brain dominants or right-brain dominants respectively, making a variety of test scores possible.

The scores might be:

- L/150 R/60 V/30 K/10
  left-brain/visual: organized and neat.

- L/160 R/40 V/0 K/40
  left-brain/kinesthetic: organized and sloppy
- L/60 R/150 V/10 K/40
  right-brain/kinesthetic: disorganized and sloppy
- L/50 R/160 V/40 K/10
  right-brain/visual: disorganized and neat

"*Sometimes*" the category we decided to include in this fourth generation questionnaire as part of the five response choices (*Always, Often, Sometimes, Rarely, Never*) presented an interesting problem: *Always* and *Often* are really a degree of the affirmative response, as *Rarely* and *Never* indicate a negative response. What then did *Sometimes* mean?

Consider Question #2: "My decisions are more spontaneous than deliberate.' Does the answer *Sometimes* suggest "yes, but the oppposite is also true?" That kind of response might indicate an Equipotential or balanced use of both hemispheres. Or, does the answer mean "I am *very* spontaneous and also *very* deliberate?" This is the opposite of the Equipotential. This type we call a Polaric Implosive. In short, this is an individual who operates at the extremes with minimal integration.

This problem with the *Sometimes* response corresponds directly to the problem of determining whether the #3 on the Neat/Sloppy rating scale is balanced between neatness and sloppiness (a mix) or a polaric swing between very neat and very sloppy.

We resolved the above problem by cautioning respondents to thoughtfully consider whether *Sometimes* was really the accurate answer for them. In many cases, *Often* or *Rarely* was the appropriate choice.

In addition, we would follow up any questionnaires in which *Sometimes* had been checked frequently with a personal interview, so that we might better understand the respondent's personality.

Evaluating The Questionnaires

We circulated 500 updated (fourth generation) questionnaires to a random sampling of men and women at shopping malls in New York and California. We asked them about their personal work habits, relationships and life-styles.

Primarily, we found that those who saw themselves as sloppy had a high right-brain/kinesthetic score and those who saw themselves as neat had a high left-brain/visual score. Our basic theory of split-brain personality clusters was valid! The neat/left-brain respondent was time conscious, logical, attentive to detail and was more deliberate in his actions. The right-brain/sloppy respondent was not time conscious, his thought process was non-sequential, he overlooked details and was spontaneous.

We chose thirty questionnaire respondents for a follow-up interview. We chose fifteen who were left-brain/visuals, and fifteen right-brain/kinesthetics. We visited them in their homes and offices to experience the nature and quality of each one's immediate environment.

It was our impression that among those who lived alone, the left-brain/visuals were more fashion-conscious with respect to clothing, more orderly in their households, more precise in their speech and adhered generally to the 'trim' body image. The right-brain/kinesthetics appeared casual in dress and their households generally look more 'lived in,' with coffee mugs, ash trays, magazines and articles of clothing scattered throughout the home. As a group, many were overweight.

Two of the activities that consistently divided the Neat from the Sloppy were dressing and undressing.

There appears to be a distinct preference among Neats and Sloppies for vertical and horizontal space. The Neats like to hang things up and the Sloppies like to lay things down.

Ida and Jules were an "odd couple" we visited one evening. Ida, who described herself as neat, gave me the following account of how she undresses every evening: "I take off one article of clothing at a time and walk over to the closet or chest where it belongs. Then I hang the item up on a hanger, or carefully fold it and place it in a drawer. The articles that need laundering are immediately thrown into the hamper. My shoes are hung on a rack behind the closet door."

This process was somewhat different for Ida's husband, Jules. "Now take my husband Jules—PLEEEASE!" Ida continued with loving exasperation: "When Jules undresses, he deposits everything he's wearing in the exact spot where he happens to be standing or sitting at the moment. In the act of disrobing, he usually manages to cover every available horizontal surface he comes in contact with. Some of his favorite target areas are the bed, the window sill, the TV set and the floor.

To this Jules responded good humoredly, "Ida certainly is neater than I am."

Ida and Jules were also a classic case of "Toothpaste Warfare." Jules said, "Ida is such a fanatic about toothpaste efficiency, that she has three wind-up devices on the bathroom counter and she is always hiding my half-used mangled tube out of sight."

The question that most consistently linked neat behavior to left-brain/visual perception and sloppy behavior to right brain/kinesthetic perception was Question #11: "I squeeze a tube of toothpaste from the bottom and replace the cap." Over 85% of those who described themselves as sloppy answered "rarely" or "never," and the same percentage of those who called themselves neat answered "always" or "often." Up to now, no one could explain why we handle toothpaste so differently. The answer, now obvious to the authors, was to be found through an understanding of the "Odd Couple Syndrome." The squeeze-it-from-the-bottom/neat person is simply responding to a left-brain/visual cue. It is *logical, sequential, linear* and *structured* to begin squeezing at the bottom of the tube. Flattening and folding the receptacle as it empties in order to get all the paste is *rational*. On the other hand, the squeeze-it-from-the-top sloppy person is *irrational, disorganized, holistic* and *sensual*. He creates the "now" experience, *immediate gratification*. Having the toothpaste at the moment, with no regard for the "future" problem of recovering the blocked-off remains, is *non-sequential*.

Questionnaire Results

The score evaluations indicated that 68% of those who filled out the questionnnaires answered an average of 15 of the 24 questions as we expected. Some questions had a higher confirming ratio than others, but this verbal differential test as a whole returned validating results. (See graphs corresponding to Questions 2, 7 and 21)

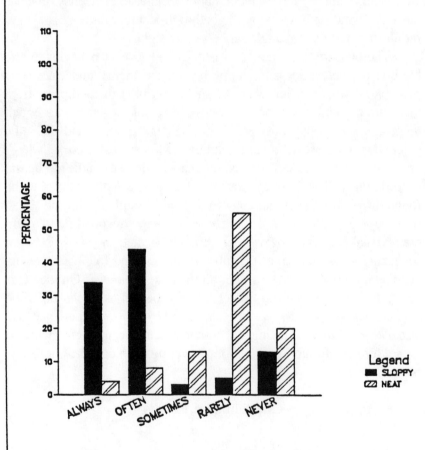

Illustration #8

I TEND TO SMOKE OR DRINK OR EAT TOO MUCH.

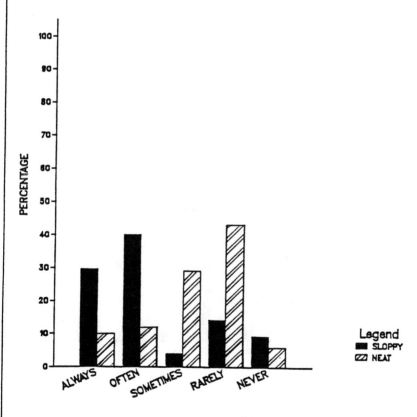

Illustration #9

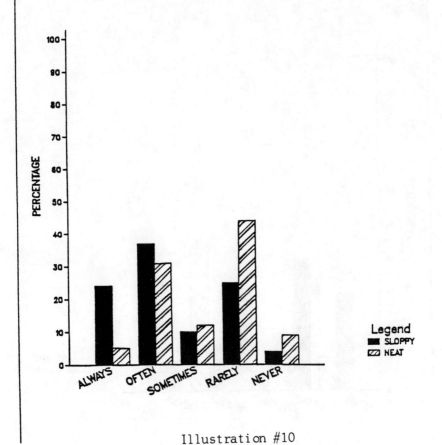

Illustration #10

Questions 1, 2, 7, 11 and 15 had the highest confirming responses, while questions 4, 6, 18 and 20 had the lowest.

Question #7—"I tend to smoke or drink or eat too much" was a high scoring right-brain question. It was our contention in designing this right-brain/kinesthetic question that the tendency to indulge one's appetite draws heavily from impulsiveness, spontaneity and the need for immediate gratification (right-brain trait) and that these potentially addictive tendencies are closely connected to the kinesthetic senses of bodily experience; we believe the high confirmation supports this assumption.

On the other hand, the results of Question #20—"I am very concerned about my physical appearance"—were inconclusive. The assumption that this would be a definitive left-brain/visual question was not substantiated. Apparently, left-brain and right-brain dominants differ little in the attention they give to their appearance.

Upon reconsideration, we have come to see that this question embodies more psychological than perceptual substance. How a person regards the importance of his physical appearance has more to do with individual early conditioning, interpersonal attitudes and self esteem than with left-brain or right-brain perceptual orientation.

Question #8, "I consider myself a saver rather than a thrower," designed as a right-brain question, received a high validating score despite the occasional confusion over the term "saver." Right-brain dominants are savers (accumulators) and left-brain dominants are throwers (discarders). Right-brain dominants tend to let things pile up (magazines, newspapers, clothes, letters, old unused furniture, broken never-to-be-repaired appliances) as they easily become attached to objects and are not concerned with the general disorder the accumulation of these items creates. Left-brain dominants tend to throw things out which have lost their function. Because of the left-brain dominant's need to organize and control the aesthetic appearance of his natural environment, he actually derives satisfaction from discarding things: it's easier than trying to find the *proper* place to store it. Some left-brain dominants told us their favorite piece of furniture is the wastepaper basket. Anything put there neither has to be filed nor later retrieved: thus, clutter is eliminated.

Some left-brain dominants were confused by the term "saver," which they took to mean "collector." "Collectors" systematically search for and acquire particular objects they catalogue, care for and display. This is an extreme left-brain activity, organized, structured and sequential in nature.

We intended the word "saver" to connote "accumulator," not "collector." In spite of the ambiguity, however, the question tested as a strong right-brain question.

We discovered that no matter how carefully one designs a verbal differential questionnaire, there always remains some room for confusion as to how each question is understood by the respondent. Although we were reasonably satisfied by the results of the questionnaire, we decided to construct another test that would demonstrate the left/right-brain dominance factor in a completely different way.

The Perceptual Differential Design Test

We constructed a test which would indicate cerebral dominance without resorting to intellectual verbal choices; this test would neither require decisions about the meaning of words nor a personal interpretation of one's own behavior. This instrument, the Perceptual Differential Design Test (PDDT), was comprised of thirteen matched pen-and-ink patterns. The respondent would have five seconds to choose between pattern (A) and pattern (B) in regard to the question, "Which design is more like me?" He would then mark a corresponding answer sheet with a check for each of the thirteen appropriately numbered boxes.

These designs were created as left-brain or right-brain forms to appeal to those aspects of a person's perception which were reflected by his own hemispheric dominance. The left-brain designs were symmetrical, rectilinear, structured, balanced and rational. The right-brain designs were asymmetrical, curvalinear, unstructured, irrational and fluid.

Our assumption was that the subject would identify with visual patterns which mirror his most common symbolic perceptual experiences: the left-brain dominant would choose more "A" designs and the RBD would choose more "B" designs.

In more than 75% of the cases where both the verbal questionnaire and the PDDT were completed, the comparative results demonstrated a positive correlation. Furthermore, the majority of left-brain dominants did indeed choose more "A" (as opposed to "B") designs on the PDDT, as did the majority of right-brain dominants choose the "B" over the "A" patterns.

The Split-Brain Eye Chart Test was constructed as a quick check to differentiate the left-brain dominant from the right-brain dominant person. This was accomplished by creating what appears to be an ordinary visual accuity test but which when read correctly carries a familiar message. The message itself is obscured because the individual letters are run on to one another so at first glance they do not appear to form words. See Illustration #11

This test was used very effectively during our workshops. A left-brain individual and a right-brained person paired up during one of the exercises were asked to view a copy of the three charts. Each diad began simultaneously. In the vast majority of cases the right-brain person accurately read the message in each chart in less time than his counterpart.

In this particular situation the right-brain person had an advantage over the left-brain person because of the ability and tendency to see the complete words in relationship to each other and therefore grasp the whole phrase.

The left-brain person was at a disadvantage because of his tendency to approach the puzzle on a linear level by trying to make sense of individual letters and individual words without grasping the sense of the phrase.

The qualities of global versus linear thinking were implicit in this test. It was useful to quickly assess left/right brain dominance. This chart also provided a check against the other methods we developed such as the questionnaire and the Perceptual Differential Design Test for determining brain dominance.

In the summer of 1983 we had the opportunity to combine a European vacation with an informal cross-cultural survey of Neat/Sloppy behavioral patterns among the English, the French, the Italians and the Spanish. The questionnaires were translated into native tongue, and with the help of friends and professionals in these countries, we managed to circulate both the questionnaire and the PDDT.

We were curious to see if the popular myths about national character would surface in this left/right brain study. It is commonly thought that the northern European countries (England, Holland, Scan-

T
HA
NKY
OUFO
RNOTS
MOKING

A
ST
ITC
HINT
IMESA
VESNINE

E
NLI
GHTE
NMENTI
STHEBES
TREVENGE

Illustration #11

dinavia, Germany, Austria) are left-brain oriented, while Southern France, Spain, Italy and Greece are right-brain oriented. One certainly gets this impression when traveling through these countries. The comparison between the prompt, clean and organized railroad system of the Swedes with that of the Italians (the latter seemed consistently late, dirty and disorganized) is a typical example.

The results of the verbal questionnaires seemed to bear out the stereotypical impression, but the PDDT exposed several contradictions. In Italy, where the dominance was considered right-brain, most of the questionnaires returned demonstrated this. But in many cases, the PDDT results were decidedly left. This was also true of those Germans who demonstrated left-brain dominance with the questionnaire and right-brain dominance with the PDDT.

Although our random sampling was not adequate enough to draw definitive conclusions about the phenomenon, it is our belief that in countries where a strong left-brain or right-brain cultural bias exists, the population will generally conform to that standard. This does not obviate the individual's own tendency toward a left-brain or right-brain perceptual style. The individual tendency would surface in the PDDT scores and most likely through the personal behavior itself.

The verbal questionnaire and the PDDT were constructed to demonstrate the correlation of brain dominance to Neatness and Sloppiness. These tests were completed by more than 1200 subjects in various parts of the United States and several European countries. In many cases, personal interviews were held in an effort to clarify test results.

By way of example, two German women we met in Northern Spain and interviewed during our tour responded to our tests. The contrast between the verbal questionnaire and the Perceptual Differential Design Test was at first baffling. Their questionnaire scores were left-brain and their PDDT scores were high right-brain. In order to understand the apparent contradiction, we did an in-depth personal interview with the two women.

We reviewed the questionnaires with each woman and found that they had given left-brain responses to a number of questions because they were motivated by cultural bias rather than their own personal feelings. On Question #10: "I have trouble keeping my personal papers up-to-date," and Question #19: "I consider hunches very important in making decisions,'' the respondents affirmed that their answers were guided by their reluctance to admit to behavior that was socially unacceptable. Upon re-evaluation, they were found to be right-brain-dominant types. What we learned from these and other respondents that we met in Europe was that a person's innate dominance is not altered by the prescribed behavior of a particular culture.

Visual/Kinesthetic Tests

In addition to the aforementioned tests, we designed an experiment/test to confirm our theory of a relationship among the visual and kinesthetic modes of consciousness and Neat and Sloppy behavior.

An interior designer and good friend generously offered the use of her living room for this experiment. The room was handsomely decorated in a contemporary style: The walls were covered with a sand-colored suede and had large floor-to-ceiling windows. Hanging plants, natural wood chairs (upholstered in cinnamon-colored leather) added to the room's ambience. Other furnishings employed earthtone colors in various, textured fabrics. A rich pile rug completed the room. We wanted to test whether, given the same environment, the visual dominant person would differ from the kinesthetic dominant in his response to the room.

Over a period of a few months we tested thirty people with this Visual Kinesthetic Test (VKT). The subject was asked to enter the room and spend about five minutes there. We then called him out and asked him a variety of questions designed to elicit his reactions to the above environment. We should add that all of those who participated in this experiment had previously completed the verbal questionnaire and the PDDT. We used these results for comparative study. Of the 15 left brain subjects, 11 gave a visually oriented response. Of the right brain group, 10 gave the kinesthetic response.

We found those who had high right-brain kinesthetic ratings on the verbal questionnaire responded ''sensorially'' to our queries about the environment: ''The room was large, very bright and sunny. It gave me a warm, comfortable feeling.'' These were typical right-brain responses, oriented toward mood, character and atmosphere. The visual person, by contrast, responded by listing the objects in the room: ''There were huge windows on the west wall, three pictures on the south wall, two were paintings of boats and the third was a seascape. There was a redwood burl coffee table in the center of the room with magazines on it.'' Here the orientation was linear: the concern was for numbers, objects and names.

It is our contention that the dominant sensory mode that one uses initially to experience an environment has a strong effect on his neatness or sloppiness. A kinesthetic individual attuned to mood and atmosphere has less concern for orderliness than for the 'feeling' the place gives him, and he is more likely to be sloppy than neat. A visually oriented individual focuses immediately on the 'arrangement' of details and is therefore more likely to be neat than sloppy.

An example of visual vs. kinesthetic perception occurred when a friend was visiting my home. David is an abstract painter and sculptor who I know to be a kinesthetic person:

Before David arrived I had had a woman clean my apartment. When she was all finished, she said, ''You know, Dr. Mills, I really worked hard today and I want to make sure that everything is the way you like it.'' I looked around and said, ''Oh, everything's fine; you did a wonderful job, thank you,'' and she left. But something was bothering me in the apartment and I suddenly realized what it was. When David arrived I asked him: ''Do you see anything strange in this apartment?'' He said, ''Strange?'' He looked around and said, ''No, it looks fine to me.''

In my living room and in my dining room I have a great many pictures hanging on the walls. Every one was tilted into a different angle, which indicated, of course, that my cleaning woman had dusted all the pictures. She had left every picture off center, and it was driving me nuts! When David looked around again, I asked: ''You don't notice anything?'' ''No,'' he replied, ''what should I notice?'' ''Look at the pictures!'' I exclaimed. ''Oh, yeah,'' he said, ''I never noticed it.'' And he went about his business. David is a classic right-brain/kinesthetic.

Synopsis of a Follow-Up Interview

The following vignette demonstrates how components of orientation, that is, the presence of left/right-brain dominance and visual/kinesthetic sensory orientation, combine to differentiate the neat person from the sloppy one. In a home interview with a young couple, Frieda and Paul, we found an extreme neat/sloppy combination.

Although this level of polarization represents a mere 20% of our sampling, it highlights the issues common to all our left/brain-brain couples.

Frieda, a social worker, received a high right-brain/kinesthetic score (160/30). She described herself as sloppy.

Paul, an attorney with a high left-brain/visual score (210/20) described himself as neat.

In response to Question 19, a right-brain/kinesthetic question ("I consider hunches very important in making decisions.") Paul answered "Never." Frieda answered "Always."

During the interview we asked Paul how he reacted when he entered a decorated room for the first time. His response: "I look around the room and see what's there, judge the quality and cost of the furnishings, and then try to decide what kind of people live there." This is a forthright example of left-brain/visual perception. Frieda's response was much different: "I never remember what is in a room, but have strong feelings about being there. Sometimes I feel very uncomfortable in a room without knowing why."

We asked Paul if there were any problems he and his wife had with Neatness and Sloppiness. Paul noted that Frieda always marred the painted walls by leaning chairs and boxes against them. This in turned forced him to spend a considerable amount of time doing touch-ups. He said he "couldn't stand to look at a house full of dirty walls."

Paul also expressed exasperation over Frieda's poor toothpaste habits and the unsightly mess she'd create by leaving wet towels and clothing on door knobs, counter tops, chairs and empty spaces of the floor.

Frieda said she never saw smudges on the walls until she saw Paul "running around with a paint brush." And as for the other complaints, she said she couldn't understand why it bothered him so much. Her main complaint was "he is always complaining."

Paul ignored that remark and went on to 'his' pet peeve. Frieda was the love of his life and the bane as well.

He said she couldn't restrain herself from squirreling away any-thing and everything that crossed their threshold. Books, newspapers and magazines were piled so high that Paul was forced to inaugurate the "set-the-limit plan." Since that memorable day whenever the limit of my tolerance is reached, I inform Frieda that she has the choice between having the item in question thrown out immediately or finding an inconspicuous place to hide it. I knew this irritated Frieda, but she agreed to abide by the rule."

At this point Frieda could not resist sharing her modus operandi in the save-or-throw game: "Do you remember when our baby sitter accidentally burnt our expensive, beautiful tea pot? The one we gave ourselves as a special anniversaary gift....It was still useable, but you threw it in the garbage, because you couldn't stand the sight of it. Then you ran out and purchased the exact same tea pot.

"I retrieved it from the garbage without telling you. A few days later you said you should have saved the cover just in case the new one became marred or chipped. I knew you disapproved of my saving things, so I never told you I had it. Now I confess to the crime of retrieving it. I have it hidden, and some day, I'll make a flower pot out of it!"

"You're teasing me! You wouldn't really do that!" Paul didn't believe a word of Frieda's story until she brought out the tea pot to prove it.

Do their opposing perceptual styles interfere with their marriage? Although the Neat/Sloppy differences were grave, the basic relationship was quite good. The interview disclosed that Paul appreciated Frieda's warmth, her effervescent nature and sexual attractiveness. He loved being with her and cared for her deeply. Frieda, in turn, expressed her appreciation for Paul's reliability, stability, orderliness and the quality of his child-rearing.

It seems opposites do attract, and that there is excitement in such a match. Apparently, the Neat/Sloppy issue need not undermine an otherwise loving relationship.

Cleaning and scrubbing can wait 'til tomorrow,
For babies grow up, we've learned to our sorrow,
So quiet down cobwebs,
Dust go to sleep,
I'm rocking my baby, and babies don't keep.
　　　　　　　　　　　—Gerty Wolfe, 1863

Chapter 6
WORKSHOP FEEDBACK

We realized our study provided a significant key to understanding and improving human relationships. We constructed a workshop so that the Odd Couple Theory might be presented to a large group. We hoped it would provide an exciting way to help people understand the differences between them.

During the past few years we've held workshops at psychology conferences, social organization meetings and college classes. From feedback of these workshops, we gathered important data from the interactions of hundreds of Neat and Sloppy people. A wealth of personal accounts and humorous stories grew out of these encounters which served to broaden and enliven our study.

The workshop consisted of lecture and experimental process. We paired groups of Neats and Sloppies who did not formerly know each other and had them go through a series of exercises to increase awareness and sensitivity to a person of the opposite perceptual orientation.

These series of exercises gave the workshop members an added perspective from which to see their own personal lives and relationships.

Below are some of the most frequently voiced criticisms and complaints Neats and Sloppies express about each other:

WHAT'S WRONG WITH NEATS	*WHAT'S WRONG WITH SLOPPIES*
Controlling	Dropping clothes
Impatient	Losing things
Too concrete	Not replacing things
Judgmental	Eating all over the house
Critical	Accumulating junk
Cheap	Cluttering horizontal surfaces
Always straightening up	Saving things
Throwing valuable things out	Always late
Obsessive	Wasting money
Pristine	Always talking on telephone
Robot-like	Irresponsible
Insensitive	Breaks promises
Workaholic	Self-indulgent
Rigid	Leaving lights on
Too cautious	Too impulsive

One workshop participant (a confessed sloppy) recalled sitting in his den, comfortably slouched in his favorite leather, wing chair reading a book, munching on cookies and drinking a cup of coffee when he felt the urge to use the bathroom. When he returned, the book, cookies, coffee were gone and the lamp table was wiped clean. He added, "I had to retrieve the book from the bookcase and refill my coffee cup, which my wife had just emptied in the kitchen sink."

An advertising copywriter who attended one of the workshops related this anecdote: "A few weeks ago the vice president of my firm, a real fanatic neatnick, issued an edict that the desk tops of all the copywriters were to be kept clear at all times. He had made an inspection of our rather 'casually' arranged writing room and I guess it upset him.

"Gradually this edict itself was smothered under piles of old notes, unread reports, magazine clippings, letters that needed answering and other material—all too important to be thrown away."

Another young man spoke of the difficulty he had keeping his New York City apartment from looking like a disaster area. He said when it becomes unbearable and he can no longer find the telephone when it rings, he goes on a cleaning binge and the apartment looks neat for about two days. "A few months ago," he said, "I came home from work and started making dinner, walking over dropped clothing, magazines, newspapers, kitty litter, dirty dishes and a pair of tennis sneakers—not noticing anything unusual. It suddenly occurred to me that I had just cleaned the apartment the day before. My apartment had been burglarized and I hadn't even realized it!"

During one workshop session, the group discussed how sexual styles of the neat and sloppy lover differed.

The left-brain dominants said that the sloppies drop their clothes everywhere, knock over lamps and ashtrays, choose inappropriate times (day or night) to make love. They initiate lovemaking in unusual places (floor, car, beach, park).

The right-brain dominants said that the neats insist on setting aside specific times and places before making love...Before getting into bed, they fold their clothes, hang them up, or put them in drawers. They brush their teeth, comb their hair and set the alarm clock for the next day before beginning the "festivities."

One neat workshop member lamented the injustice of the left-brain dominant predicament: "You can't get anything clean without getting something else dirty, but you can get everything dirty without getting anything clean."

One woman spoke of her twenty-two-year-old fraternal twins, Madeline and Byron, whom she described as different tempermentally from birth. As infants, Madeline was restless and moody while Byron was placid and malleable. Madeline was interested in dance, painting and literature and was noted for her fine short story writing. Byron was an excellent science and mathematics student who went on to a career in computer engineering. During the course of the workshop, the woman made remarks such as, "I was astonished at how much my children's personalities paralleled with the left-brain/right-brain dichotomy. Madeline was always sloppy and always late.

"Byron was neat and organized to a fault and would rather be ten minutes early for an appointment than two minutes late.

"When you gave us the perceptual design test, it reminded me that Madeline doodles with circles and curved lines, while Byron would doodle with rectangles and straight lines."

This is not an isolated account. Similar information has come to our attention which points up that some children with similar environment show opposite orientation.

The striking features of this woman's account, however, is that the children were fraternal twins and shared a similar environment with respect to birth order and parenting, and yet they developed antipodal, perceptual orientations.

Chapter 7
Research Background
For The Odd Couple Syndrome

Free from any preconceptions about the origin of this strange phenomenon of Neat/Sloppy behavior, our quest took us through a labyrinth of assumptions, speculations and hunches, and then scientific data, testing and surveys which eventually led us to the original theory of the Odd Couple Snydrome.

The only significant theory on Neat/Sloppy behavior we found was Sigmund Freud's doctrine of anal fixation. Freud believed that neatness and sloppiness resulted from parental handling of the issue of gratification and conflict during the child's period of toilet training.

It is surprising that the last definitive psychological work on the topic of Neat/Sloppy behavior was done more than seventy years ago. In 1910, Freud divided child development into five psychosexual stages (Oral, Anal, Phallic, Latent, and Genital). He selected the Anal stage as the source of all Neat/Sloppy problems. He believed that the way parents handle the issue of toilet training determines the development of the Anal retentive character (neat) and the Anal expulsive character (sloppy): "The anal-erotic drives meet in infancy with the training for cleanliness and the way in which this training is carried out determines whether or not anal fixations result. The training may be too early, too late, too strict, too erotic. Some people as infants refuse to empty their bowels when they are put on the pot because they derive a subsidiary pleasure from defecating. We can infer that such people are born with a sexual constitution in which the erotogenicity of the anal zone is exceptionally strong."[1]

According to Freud, the anal retentive is inclined toward a neat, orderly style of life. His deep need is to avoid any implication that he does not have secure control of his anal functions. This, said Freud, is accomplished by exaggerated efforts to represent oneself as religiously putting things in the right place, and by being predictable, precise and trustworthy. The anal expulsive, on the other hand, is the rebel, the one who refuses to be trained. The expulsive exhibits all the opposite behavioral patterns. He is untidy, disorganized, tardy and irresponsible.

Over the last forty years many psychologists have sought to substantiate Freudian theories by subjecting them to scientific testing. Researchers during this period have administered multiple tests to subjects and factor-analyzed them to ascertain whether there are in fact definable anal groupings. With few exceptions, the tests have consisted of questionnaires that ask the individual to indicate how he relates to others, what activities he prefers and his general style of behavior. The following is a brief overview of the character traits explored in these factor-analytic studies:

Sears (1943)	the relationship among ratings of orderliness, stinginess and stubbornness;
Barnes (1952)	orderliness, meticulousness, reliability, cleanliness law abidance;
Stagner (1955)	giving things away, doing for others, collecting stamps, promptness, buying bargins and preserving things.
Beloff (1957)	tardiness, the lending of books and other possessions.
Mandel (1958)	generosity, concern with dirt, cleanliness, collecting things, punctuality, interest in details.
Finney (1961)	compulsiveness, orderliness, stinginess and ridigity.
Schlessinger (1963)	responsibility, meticulousness, obstinacy.
Comrey (1965)	need for order, love of routine, cautiousness.

Lazare (1966)   orderliness, perseverance, emotional constriction.
Kline (1968)   hypocrisy, submission to authority, hoarding,
                       conservatism.

These past studies have almost unanimously found it possible to isolate recognizable clusters of character traits.

Freud's ability to group certain types of behavior together to form a *retentive* or *expulsive* character cluster was indeed a testament to his genius, *but his assumption that these qualities were linked to the stage of anal development and specifically to toilet training has never been authenticated*. Nevertheless, a number of studies have tried to establish a tie between the two. They are:

Huschka (1942)	Holway (1949)	Whiting & Child (1953)
Sewell (1953)	Prugh (1954)	Bernstein (1955)
Straus (1957)	Stein (1953)	Durrett (1958)
Hetherington &	Sears (1965)	Miller & Swanson (1966)
Blackbill (1963)		Kline (1969).

Psychiatrist Seymour Fisher, in his book *The Scientific Credibility of Sigmund Freud*, reviewed twenty experimental studies that have tried to establish a tie between toilet training practices and anal attributes. He writes: "Sifting through the disparate findings one is *forced to conclude* there is little support for the hypothesis that a child's toilet training determines whether he will manifest three traits (orderliness, obstinancy, parsimony) Freud linked with anality."[2]

Two psychological researchers, Whiting and Child (1953) discovered, after analysis of several cultures, that the nature of toilet training in each was not meaningfully correlated to anal attributes. In fact, they were surprised to find that the apparent limited effect of toilet training upon the individual's anal retention contrasted strongly with other behaviors not included in the anal syndrome. They reported that rigid toilet training resulted in enhanced femininity in girls and diminished masculinity in boys among Singhalese children.[3]

Freud believed we are all driven from within by Eros and that what seems to be higher motives are merely disguised versions of Eros. His fellows took issue with him but retained the idea of the singular motivation. Adler (1956) substituted the seeking of power as primary. Sullivan (1940) saw social solidarity as basic and Fromm (1941) has us searching after self, but all believed that men are fundamentally alike and that their personalities are shaped solely by the variety of their environmental experiences.[4]

Carl Jung (1923) disagreed. He argued that people are different in fundamental ways. He points to character types which do not alter from birth to death, namely, the Introvert and the Extrovert. The main trait of the Introvert is being "inner-directed," whereas that of the Extrovert is being "outer-directed." An Introvert directs his mind, thought, and effort inward. An Extrovert directs his interest to external objects and people and actions.[5]

The belief that people are alike appears to be a twentieth century notion related most likely to the growth of democracy in the Western World. If we are equals then we must be alike.

The concept of polarities among individuals appealed to us as a way of thinking about the Neat/Sloppy split, so we complied a list of opposites to see if we could identify any significant connections between them.

Introvert	Extrovert
Winner	Loser
Materialist	Idealist
Yin	Yang
Giver	Taker
Artist	Craftsman
NEAT	SLOPPY
Romantic	Classical
Left/Brain	Right/Brain

It occured to us that many of the artists we knew were sloppy, and that I, a serious craftsman (photographer, furniture finisher) am neat. A cursory recollection of our friends and acquaintances confirmed this curious parallel.

To further test our theory that artists are sloppy and craftsmen are neat, we attended art shows and crafts fairs to interview individuals of these professions.

We arbitrarily defined art as "that which is pursued for emotional expression," and craft as "that which is practiced to produce an object of function." Of course, we do find art which has less emotional impact on the observer than a well-crafted cabinet, but we're interested in how artists and craftsmen approach their respective tasks, not necessarily the quality of their creations. Over a period of two months we interviewed forty artists and craftsmen. We found that the overwhelming majority of artists were sloppy and that most craftsmen were neat.

We asked them to evaluate themselves as neat or sloppy in their work and home settings and to describe their work process. The composite sketch we gleaned was that the craftsman carefully thinks out a project step-by-step, assembles materials, researches various methods of approach and then proceeds to work. Most artists start with an inspiration, an image or some intuitive feeling, without having a precise plan. Only a small percentage of each group did not fit this mode. Some of the artists worked like craftsmen and vice versa.

The pieces were slowly beginning to fit together. We explored in depth the relationships among thinking styles, perception and the Neat/Sloppy phenomenon. Soon it became clear that it is not *attitude*, as many think, that creates the dichotomy between Neat and Sloppy, it is *perception*. It is not a neurotic fixation, but rather that we experience the same reality from two different perspectives. The neat and the sloppy person each sees the world in a different way. And it was this line of reasoning that led us into the voluminous literature of Split-Brain research.

Split-Brain Research

Research findings in hemisphericity confirm something which we have always known and which both Western and Eastern writers have described: there exists a duality in human mental processing—the effect of which is that individuals have two distinct approaches to learning, remembering and thinking.

Hypocrates, Father of Medicine, believed that thought and emotion originated in the brain, not in the heart as his contemporaries believed. He noted that a wound to the left side of the head affected the right side of the body and vice versa. He wisely concluded that "the brain of man is double."[6]

The fascination with understanding brain function and localization persisted throughout the centuries to follow. French author Marcel Proust wrote: "We feel in one world; we think, we give names to

Illustration #12

THE TWO KINDS OF CONSCIOUSNESS

Observed by	Left brain related	Right brain related
Akhilinanda	buddi	manas
Assagioli	intellect	intuition
Austin	convergent	divergent
Bacon	argument	experience
Bateson & Jackson	digital	analogic
Blackburn	intellectual	sensuous
Bogen	propositional	appositional
Bronowski	deductive	imaginative
Bruner	rational	metaphoric
Cohen	analytic	relational
De Bono	vertical	horizontal
Deikman	active	receptive
Dieudonne	discrete	continuous
Freud	secondary	primary
Goldstein	abstract	concrete
Guilford	convergent	divergent
Hilgard	relatistic	impulsive
Hobbes	directed	free
Humphrey & Zangwill	propositional	imaginative
I Ching	the creative	the receptive
	masculine	feminine
	Yang	Yin
	light	dark
	time	space
James	differential	existential
Jung	causal	acausal
Kagan & Moss	analytic	relational
Lee	lineal	nonlineal
Levi-Strauss	positive	mythic
Levy & Sperry	analytic	gestalt
Lomas & Berkowitz	differentiation	integration
Loye	serial time	spatial time
	inferential intuition	gestalt intuition
Luria	sequential	simultaneous
McFie, Piercy	relations	correlates
McKellar	realistic	autistic
Maslow	rational	intuitive
Mills	neat	sloppy
Neisser	sequential	multiple
Oppenheimer	historical	timeless
Ornstein	analytic	holistic
Pavlov	second signal	first signal
Peirce	explicative	ampliative
Polanyi	explicit	tacit
Price	reductionist	compositionist
Radhakrishnan	rational	integral
Reusch	discursive	eidetic
Schenov	successive	simultaneous
Schopenhauer	objective	subjective
Semmes	focal	diffuse
Smith	atomistic	gross
Wells	hierarchical	heterarchical

adapted from lists originally compiled by Joseph Bogen and Robert Ornstein

by David Loye

things in another; between the two we can establish correspondence but we do not bridge the internal.'' Rudyard Kipling, in a poem entitled *The Two Sided Man* writes:

> "I would go without shirt or shoe,
> Friend, tobacco or bread,
> Sooner than lose for a minute the two
> Separate sides of my head!''

The nineteenth century saw important advances in the study of split-brain research. Dr. Broca discovered and documented the localization of the main speech area in the left frontal lobe (Broca's Area). Dr. Wernicke did similar work with language comprehension in the left temporal lobe (Wernicke's Area). But it was not until the 1950s, when several technical advances permitted more sophisticated studies of brain functioning, that new breakthroughs in brain research were made.

Since the nineteenth century, neurologists and brain surgeons have noted that tumors and excisions within the left hemisphere of the brain produce quite different effects on the patient's mental abilities than do the tumors within the right hemisphere. Damage to the left side of the brain has long been associated with aphasia (loss of speech) while damage to the right hemisphere disturbs the patient's sense of body orientation. The latter neither can dress himself nor recognize familiar faces.

Neurologists saw that damage to the left hemisphere impedes speech, language, verbal memory, mathematical ability and one's sense of time. Damage to the right hemisphere impedes performance in understanding visual and tactile mazes, perception of depth and movement, spatial organization and tends to produce general patterns of disturbance.

A major breakthrough occurred in the field of brain research in the early 1960s. The research was executed mainly by Roger W. Sperry and Michael Gazzaniga at the California Institute of Technology.

Sperry experimented primarily on the brains of cats. He and his assistants cut the corpus callosum between the right and left hemisphere of the cerebral cortex. Through a series of careful experiments, they found that the cats were now operating with two entirely separate self-contained and mostly self-sufficient brains within a single skull. Neurosurgeon Joseph Bogen, who was familiar with the work being done by the Sperry team, theorized that this operation might provide relief for patients with certain kinds of epilepsy.

A group of patients who had been disabled by epileptic seizures involving both cerebral hemispheres applied for this most innovative neurological procedure. The operations were performed by Drs. Joseph Bogen and Phillip Vogel. They severed the corpus callosum (a nerve cable composed of millions of fibers that cross-connect the two cerebral hemispheres) completely isolating the right brain from the left brain. The operations were extremely successful in controlling the seizures and the patients made complete recoveries.

And so Bogen's hunch proved correct! He not only helped the patients, but he opened the floodgates to the study of right-left brain differences. For the first time in history, there was a group of people with separated brains who were available for scientific investigation.

The Cal Tech group subsequently worked with these patients in a series of ingenious tests that revealed the separated functions of the two hemispheres. The tests revealed new evidence that each hemisphere perceives reality in its own way, the left brain with its verbal, analytic time sequential mode, and the right brain with its rapid, whole pattern spatial, non-rational mode.[7]

What surprised the surgeons were the apparently small effects of so major an operation. It took a series of carefully constructed experiments to reveal that there are two separate minds within the human brain: a left hemisphere controlling the right side of the body and a right hemisphere controlling the left side of the body.

In one experiment, a patient who had undergone the split-brain operation was given a pencil to hold in his right hand where he could not see it. He was asked to describe what it was he held. He responded "a pencil," since the right hand connects to the verbal left hemisphere. But, when the pencil was placed in the left hand, the silent right hemisphere was unable to instruct the left and so he could not describe the pencil.

In 1962, Roger Sperry, who in 1981 received the Nobel Prize for his ground-breaking work in split-brain research, along with Neuropsychologist Michael Gazzaniga, constructed an apparatus which allowed separate communications with each half of the patient's brain. Words or pictures could be shown to one hemisphere only by projecting them briefly on the left or the right side of the screen. Below the screen was a slot for the hands so that objects could be felt with one hand without being seen by the other hemisphere.

See Illustration #13

Further experiments demonstrated other communicative difficulties. The words "hat band" were flashed on the screen so that "hat" was on the right hemisphere and "band" was on the left. When asked what word he saw the subject replied "band." When asked what kind of band, he made all sorts of guesses-"rubber band, rock band, band of robbers," etc. What is perceived by the right hemisphere does not transfer over to the left in the conscious awareness of the split-brain subject. With the corpus callosum severed, each hemisphere seems oblivious to the experiences of the other. See Illustration #14

Research has now gone far beyond these early experiments to reveal hemispheric specialization in normal subjects. Biofeedback instruments, which register the degree of electric discharge from brain cells, show increased alpha rhythms in whichever hemisphere is at rest, and an increased electric discharge in the hemisphere that is at work. Ask someone a verbal or mathematical problem and the left begins to fire. Present him with a video-spatial problem and the right hemisphere fires. Eye movement also correlates with hemispheric specialization.

A typical eye movement experiment was reported by Raquel & Rubin Gur of Stanford University[8]. They asked 49 male college students verbal and spatial questions while a hidden television camera recorded their eye movements. The verbal questions required verbal explanations of proverbs such a "Rome was not built in a day" or "All that glitters is not gold." The spatial questions such as those below all required internal visualization: "Visualize sitting in front of a typewriter"; "Where is the letter 'R' relative to the letter 'B'?"; or "Where is Chicago relative to Minneapolis?" When the results were tabulated it was found that the eye moved to the right 64% of the time after the verbal questions and to the left 69% of the time after spatial questions.[8]

In the late 1950s and early 60s, a team of Russian neurophysiologists led by Vadim L. Deglin tested a group of patients

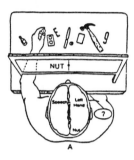
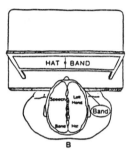

Illustration #14

Testing the abilities of the two hemispheres

A. The split-brain subject correctly retrieves an object by touch with the left hand when its name is flashed to the right hemisphere, but he cannot name the object or describe what he has done. B. The word "hatband" is flashed so that "hat" goes to the right cerebral hemisphere and "band" goes to the left hemisphere. The subject reports that he sees the word "band" but has no idea what kind of band. C. A list of common objects (including book and cup) is initially shown to both hemispheres. One word from the list (book) is then projected to the right hemisphere. When given the command to do so, the left hand begins writing the word "book," but when questioned the subject doesn't know what his left hand has written and guesses "cup." (After Sperry, 1970; and Nebes and Sperry, 1971)

from Introduction to psychology
Hilgard, Atkinson, Atkinson

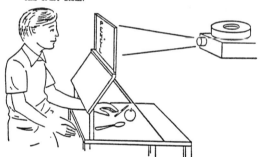

THE SPLIT BRAIN

The classical split-brain experiment: While the subject stares at a spot in the center of the screen, a word or picture is flashed on one side of the screen only. In the example shown, only the patient's right hemisphere will see the word "pencil." He will therefore be verbally unable to indicate what he saw, but his left hand will be able to select the pencil from the group of objects.

from the Right Brain
Thomas R. Blakeslee

Illustration #13

who had just had unilateral shock treatments. This was a variation of shock therapy the Russians developed for the treatment of depression. Only one side of the brain received the grand-mal inducing electrodes, thus causing much less confusion and trauma for the patient. Instead of falling into a complete stupor, the patient temporarily became a "left-brain person" or a "right-brain person," depending on which side of the brain received the treatment. The effect was as if the patient had a temporary hemispherectomy.

After electroshock to the right hemisphere, the patient's left hemisphere was more active, having been liberated from competition with the right. The patient became more talkative, sometimes to excess. His vocabulary became richer and more eclectic and his answers were more elaborate. His intonation, however, became less expressive, more monotonous, in short, colorless and dull. A similar defect was observed in the patient's sensitivity to voice tone. The left hemisphere by itself cannot detect things such as anger, playfulness or enthusiasm as are communicated by intonation. When recordings of natural sounds such as coughing, laughter, snoring and crashing waves were played, the patient had difficulty identifying them. Often, the left hemisphere would classify the sound rather than identify it. Instead of saying "that's a dog barking," the patient would say, "that's an animal." Often, the classification would be wrong, but the mere propensity to classify is indigenous to left-hemisphere orientation.

Visual perception was also impaired without the help of the right hemisphere. When asked to match pairs of simple geometric figures such as triangles, squares, etc., the patient was unable to do it if the figures were covered with confusing colored or striped sectors. Here we have a magnification of the classic problem of the inability to "see the forest for the trees." Though the patient could name the hospital, ward number, and other "verbal" details, his visual recognition of his whereabouts was clearly impaired. He looked in bewilderment at the consulting room which he had frequented and insisted he had never been there before. While he could easily memorize and recite new verbal material, he was unable to memorize and identify those shapes not easily given a verbal label. Sometimes the "left hemisphere person" could not decide whether it was winter by simply looking out of the window at the snowdrifts and bare trees. He might deduce that it was winter because the month was January, but the simple visual impression escaped him.

Generally, the emotional outlook of these patients was easygoing and cheerful, albeit their normal state saw a pattern of chronic depression or preoccupation with their illness. It appears then that the left brain is basically optimistic and cheerful, even when the reality of the individual's situation is depressing.

When a patient received shock therapy on the left side only, making him temporarily a "right hemisphere person," his emotional outlook became morose and pessimistic about his present situation and his future. His speech activity was greatly reduced. Instead of answering questions in words, he preferred to respond by mime or by gestures. He often became silent after briefly answering one or two questions. The speech of this "right-hemisphere person" showed a sharply dimished vocabulary and did not include words for abstract concepts. He had difficulty recalling names of objects, especially those infrequently used, but he could explain the purpose of any object or demonstrate its use. His speech was marked by simplistic sentence structure and often by isolated words. But the precision of his capacity to hear nonverbal sounds was excellent and he was better at perceiving natural sounds such as the crashing surf than he would have been with both halves of his brain functioning. He recognized music immediately and would tend to hum along without even being asked. Apparently, the lack of competition from the left brain improved his performance of these tasks. Matching geometric shapes covered with confusing colors was no problem for the "right-hemisphere person." Spotting missing details on pictures and memorizing complex shapes were likewise easy. He could look out of the window and immediately determine the season.[9]

In addition to studying the right/left separation of the inner mental experience, the scientists examined the different ways in which the two hemispheres process information. Evidence accumulated to show that the mode of the left hemisphere is verbal and analytic, while that of the right is nonverbal and global. New evidence found by Neuro-psychologist Jerre Levy showed that the mode of processing used by the right brain is rapid, complex, whole-pattern, and spatial; and the perceptual-processing is not only different from the complexity of the left brain's verbal analytic mode, but comparable as well.[10]

The left brain tends to think in a consecutive one-step-at-a-time manner, while the right brain uses a parallel approach. This difference in processing strategy was demonstrated in normal individuals by measuring their reaction time to a task when presented to the left or right visual field. The task in this case was to recognize whether a given word belonged to a set of words previously memorized. Subjects were asked to press a "yes" or "no" button as soon as they knew whether the word was one of those memorized. When the word was flashed to the right visual field, reaction time increased as the number of words in the memorized set increased. This shows that the left brain was using the serial approach of comparing the words seen one-at-a-time with each of the words memorized. Using this approach, of course, the more words there are to compare, the longer it takes to react. When the words was flashed to the left visual field, time was the same no matter how many words were in the memorized set. The right brain thus appeared to have been using a parallel approach in which the decision was made without examining each word separately. When the list of things to be remembered increased (as in face picture recognition) this approach became indispensible.[11]

In 1972, David Galin and Robert Ornstein (University California Medical Center) tried recording EEG signals from the left and right side of the brain separately while the subject did verbal or spatial tasks. The result confirmed that normal individuals tend to think with either one side of the brain or the other. When the subject did a verbal task, the alpha rhythm was reduced on the left side but remained on the right. The right brain thus continued to idle while the left brain worked on the problem. Spatial tasks produced the opposite result, indicating right-brain processing.[12]

All the foregoing research and exploration into the functioning of the split-brain over the past thirty years has laid a new foundation from which to view human behavior. If indeed man's brain is double and each side has its own unique way of thinking, experiencing and understanding, then it is important to consider how each hemisphere is used, for what tasks, and whether the process is the same for everyone.

The following lists of left and right brain characteristics clearly delineate the polaric nature of the two hemispheres of the cerebral cortex. SEE ILLUSTRATION # 14

The current state of brain research suggests, according to Jerre Levy, that "the human cerebral hemispheres exist in a symbiotic relationship in which both the capacities and motivations to act are complementary. Each side of the brain is able to perform and chooses to perform a certain set of cognitive tasks which the other side finds difficult or distasteful or both. The right hemisphere synthesizes over space. The left hemisphere analyzes over time. The right hemisphere codes sensory input in terms of images, the left in terms of linguistic descriptions. The right hemisphere lacks an analyzer, the left hemisphere lacks a pattern synthesizer."[13]

Do our left and right brains alternate in their response to the environment, one resting while the other is employed, depending on the nature of the stimulus? Or, do they function simultaneously, each processing out of the total situation those facets they do best? Or are our two brains pitted against each other in a constant battle for "executive control?" Most of the time our brains apparently act in perfect harmony, transferring information and thought smoothly across the nerve currents of the corpus callosum, from hemisphere to hemisphere, resulting in synchronized behavior. Divisions of labor and consequent differences in brain organization do exist, however, despite man's perception of the mind as a singular whole.

Some researchers think the two hemispheres actually do compete to determine our overriding styles of cognition in life. They feel we tend to favor the function of one hemisphere or the other in our mental behavior, that as thinkers we are apt to be either verbal and symbolic, or perceptive and imagistic.

Dr. Gerald Turkewitz, a psychologist at the Albert Einstein School of Medicine, speculates that many aspects of the right/left-hemisphere specialization begin before birth and are genetically programmed.[14] Raquel and Rubin Gur, a husband and wife team of psychologists (University of Pennsylvania) studied adult personality traits associated

**Abbreviated summary of specialized cerebral hemisphere functions in terms of styles of learning and thinking

LEFT	RIGHT
Recognizing/remembering names	Recognizing/remembering faces
Responding to verbal instructions	Responding to visual and kinestheti instructions
Systematic and controlled in experimenting/learning/thinking	Playful and loose in experimenting/ learning/thinking
Inhibited emotionally	Responds with emotion/feeling
Dependent upon words for meaning	Interprets body language easily
Produces logical ideas/thoughts	Produces humorous ideas/thoughts
Processes verbal stimuli	Processes kinesthetic stimuli
Processes information logically	Processes information subjectively
Serious, systematic, planful in solving problems	Playful in solving problems, uses humor, experiments
Receptive; abstract thinking	Self acting; concrete thinking
Likes to have definite plan	Likes to improvise
Not psychic	Highly psychic
Little use of metaphors and analogies	Frequent use of metaphors and analogies
Responsive to logical, verbal appeals	Responsive to emotional appeals
Deals with one problem at a time, sequentially	Deals simultaneously with several problems at a time
Critical and analytical in reading, listening	Creative, synthesizing, associating applying in reading
Logical in solving problems	Intuitive in solving problems
Gives instruction/information verbally	Gives much information through movement, gesture
Uses language in remembering	Uses images in remembering
Grasps certain, established truths	Grasps new, uncertain truths
Linear (clock) time	Non linear (organic) time

**from Torrance, E. Paul, *Your Style of Learning and Thinking*
Department of Educational Psychology
University of Georgia; Athens, Georgia, July, 1977

Illustration #15

Drawing on the Right Side of the Brain by Betty Edwards

―――――――――― Illustration #16 ――――――――――

A Comparison of Left-Mode and Right-Mode Characteristics

 – MODE

 – MODE

Verbal: Using words to name, describe, define.

Nonverbal: Awareness of things, but minimal connection with words.

Analytic: Figuring things out step-by-step and part-by-part.

Synthetic: Putting things together to form wholes.

Symbolic: Using a symbol to *stand for* something. For example, the drawn form ◑ stands for *eye*, the sign + stands for the process of addition.

Concrete: Relating to things as they are, at the present moment.

Abstract: Taking out a small bit of information and using it to represent the whole thing.

Analogic: Seeing likenesses between things; understanding metaphoric relationships.

Temporal: Keeping track of time, sequencing one thing after another: Doing first things first, second things second, etc.

Nontemporal: Without a sense of time.

Rational: Drawing conclusions based on *reason* and *facts*.

Nonrational: Not requiring a basis of reason or facts; willingness to suspend judgment.

Digital: Using numbers as in counting.

Spatial: Seeing where things are in relation to other things, and how parts go together to form a whole.

Logical: Drawing conclusions based on logic: one thing following another in logical order — for example, a mathematical theorem or a well-stated argument.

Intuitive: Making leaps of insight, often based on incomplete patterns, hunches, feelings, or visual images.

Linear: Thinking in terms of linked ideas, one thought directly following another, often leading to a convergent conclusion.

Holistic: Seeing whole things all at once; perceiving the overall patterns and structures, often leading to divergent conclusions.

with right/left eye movers. They concluded that gaze direction in response to questions is determined by problem type and by the individual's characteristic tendency to use a certain hemisphere.[15]

"If indeed left and right movers differ in a tendency to rely on one or the other hemisphere, one would expect them to show corresponding differences in their characteristic modes of coping with problems and conflict." Raquel Gur further suggested that those with a tendency to look to the left might be expected to be more holistic and nonverbal in their response to stress. Right-movers in contrast, might be more analytic and intellectual in their approach to a problem.

For this hypothesis, the Gurs evaluated twenty-eight men with clear-cut eye-movement performances and found that the majority of the "left-movers" leaned towards a right-hemisphere style of thinking while "right-movers" exhibited a decided propensity for left-hemisphere style.

The importance of the Gurs' eye-movement studies stems from the light shed on how we all differ in our tendency to preferentially use one or the other of our hemispheres, thereby developing a dominant cognitive style.[15]

Odd Couple Syndrome Theory

The impetus for this study, as you may recall, was a hunch that the thinking styles of the artist/craftsman somehow held a key to understanding the Neat/Sloppy dichotomy. Further on in our research, it became clear that left/right brain research would provide the main foundation for the "Odd Couple" theory.

The craftsman thinks in analytical, linear, sequential step-by-step procedures directed toward a specific goal. These are the characteristic qualities of the left brain. The artist thinks in metaphors, images, spatial concepts and intuitive leaps of insight. We believe it is exactly these antipodal qualities, the outer-directedness (left-brain) and inner-directedness (right-brain) that create the perceptual orientation as evidenced in the Neat/Sloppy phenomenon.

The Neat (or left-brained) person is concerned with structure, organization and visual order; he is detail conscious and sequentially oriented. The Sloppy (or right-brained) person has no concern for object organization; he is more attuned to the immediate experience of simultaneous patterns than linear, sequential ones.

If a neat person and a sloppy person were both confronted with the task of planning a dinner party for six, each would handle it in his own characteristic way: The neat person would list all necessary arrangements and purchases (structured); decide what to do first, second and third (sequential); have all his cooking equipment and recipes available for immediate use (organized); and assess how much time each task requires (time conscious). The sloppy person would have a picture in his mind of what the party would be like (images); try to do several things at once (simultaneous); wonder where he put the broiler rack and whatever happenèd to that gourmet cookbook (disorganized); and spend the time alloted for preparation on the telephone chatting with friends (timeless).

Both modes of behavior might very well produce a successful dinner party although by a very different process. We think that here it is important to acknowledge that all average healthy individuals have two hemispheres which operate all the time, negotiating the simplest to the most complex of life's tasks, and that there are no completely right-brain or left-brain individuals. But it is generally accepted amongst researchers in the field that most of us tend to favor the use of one hemisphere over the other (left-brain dominant versus right-brain dominant). For a variety of reasons (genetic, environmental, psychological), we tend to perceive the world in one of two ways. The degree of dominance naturally will vary from one person to another.

Although split-brain research and left/right-brain perceptual styles formed the major cornerstone of the "Odd Couple Syndrome," it did leave some aspects of the phenomenon unexplained.

The second part of this exploration into the origin of the Neat/Sloppy behavior rests on the ground-breaking work by Richard Bandler, a Gestalt therapist, and John Grinder, a linguist, who together developed the theory of Neuro-Linguistic Programming. They argued that all human communication styles are reducible to three major sensory modes: Visual, Auditory and Kinesthetic. Most of us use all three modes in varying degrees at different times, but almost everyone has a predominant order of sensory intake. A visual dominant individual responds to all the information he sees; an auditory dominant individual is affected most by what he hears; and a kinesthetic dominant individual picks up most of his information from his feelings.

Split-hemispheric functioning explains how we organize the information we bring into our organism (left-brain analytic, logical, or right-brain intuitive, abstract or left/right integrative) but neurolinguistics explains how we *acquire* that information. Although everyone uses all three sensory modes, they are expressed within each of us in a different order of dominance.

One person will respond primarily to what he sees (visual) while another will respond more strongly to what he feels and senses(kinesthetic). When we saw how the senses fit into the process of perception, we were able to complete the matrix that forms our basic theory.

We designed a four-part matrix of interlacing factors to describe the Neat/Sloppy person. This consisted of left-brain/right-brain, visual/kinesthetic functioning. We predicted that the composition of each individual with respect to the combinations of the various processes would relate directly to Neat/Sloppy behavior.

Our theory then is as follows: An individual who primarily gathers environmental information visually and processes it mainly in his left brain will be neat; one who primarily gathers information kinesthetically and processes it mainly in his right brain will be sloppy.

The other two categories of right-brain/visual and left-brain / kinesthetic are much smaller in number. One who experiences the world visually but processes it in his right brain will be neat in the way he arranges things aesthetically, but disorganized in the way he keeps order. This type of person may have an orderly apartment but have disorganized closests and messy filing cabinets. Closets, messy filing records and trouble keeping appointments are some examples. One who collects information kinesthetically and processes it in the left brain will be sloppy in the way he arranges things aesthetically, yet organized in storing his clothes and keeping records. He will always find things he is looking for. See Illustration #17

It is the interaction between the right/left brain functions and the visual/kinesthetic sensory modes that creates the experience which determines an individual's approach to his material environment. If a person is left-brain dominant and experiences most of his environmental information visually, he will be highly conscious of the physical appearance of things and concerned about their arrangement and organization.

The right brain dominant kinesthetic person is more attuned to the impulse, to feelings, to immediate gratification and to comfort. In the home, for example, when faced with the choice of either dropping clean laundry on the bed or taking a few minutes to fold and put it away, he will more often than not opt for the former. The left-brain dominant visual person, whose concern is for structure and

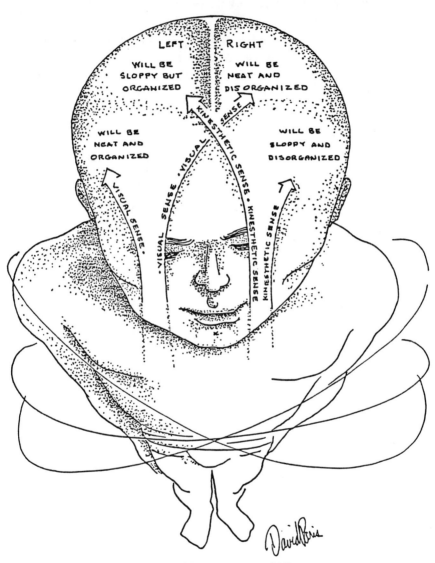

Illustration #17

order, attends to the visual experience. He will usually fold the laundry and put everything in its place because he cares how things will look and because he is time-oriented.

It should be no surprise that we often choose mates of the opposite perceptual style, unconsciously recognizing qualities in them that we want for ourselves. These relationships are potentially stimulating and fulfilling, but they often enter the formidable zone of the Odd Couple Syndrome.

In Acceptance, Appreciation and Accommodation we have a formula to insure more harmony in an ''Odd Couple'' relationship. In fact, it is in this very interaction between the partners of an ''Odd Couple'' that we have a metaphor for the integration of the individual's own split consciousness. And so the cleaning up of the Neat/Sloppy conflict is also a step toward a more integrated self.

Chapter 8
Odd Couple Theory
and Psychotherapy

The science of human behavior is flooded with hundreds of conflicting personality theories, each declaring itself the definitive truth. But, it has been our experience as psychotherapists that very little about human personality can be deemed absolute. Most of these theories have been developed without any understanding of how the brain, our major thinking organ, operates. Neuro-psychologists are now just beginning to unravel some of the complex mysteries surrounding the human brain.

Despite its masquerade as a unified organ, its thinking processes are governed by the two different styles of the left and right hemisphere. Each hemisphere appears to have its own separate and private sensations, its own perceptions, its own concepts, its own active and reactive impulses. Many of us move in and out of these two modes at various periods of our lives and during different activities, but we adhere to a familiar mode of consciousness which reflects itself in left or right dominant behavior.

Much has been written pro and con regarding the validity of the left/right brain personality paradym. It is not surprising that a new theory of this magnitude should stimulate controversy among psychologists, neurologists, educators and philosophers.

Some dismiss the "left/right brain thing" as a fad and others embrace it as an answer to all the mysteries of the human mind.

Historically, every major new discovery in a scientific field will find detractors among those who fear threatening implications to their own established views.

We consider the left/right concept an essential component of any psychological theory seeking to understand human behavior. It does not replace, invalidate or compete with any of the existing schools of personality theory but rather is an underlying factor, long overlooked, which informs, explains and enriches every system.

Ultimately, the validity of any new theory is determined by time and the usefulness it serves to enhance the larger body of knowledge. Nevertheless, the importance of the left/right brain study has been highlighted by the presentation of the Nobel Prize to Roger Sperry for his groundbreaking work in this field. Dr. David Loye of UCLA Medical School and Dr. Sid J. Segalowitz of Brock University, Ontario, two distinguished researchers engaged in these studies for many years concur that discoveries in brain-functional differences and their application to human psychology have only begun to scratch the surface.

David Galin of The Langley Porter Neuropsychiatric Institute and Dr. Klaus Hoppe of UCLA Medical School have suggested that the discoveries in brain lateralization may be an explanation of Freud's concept of primary and secondary process. Indeed, Laurence Miller, Professor of Neuropsychology at Seton Hall University, sees the expanding study of left/right brain research as a source of scientific vindication for many of Freud's ideas about human psychology.

As psychotherapists, we have practiced over the years with a fair measure of success. Although our training and orientations were different (Max's background was psychoanalytic and mine was Gestalt), we both intuitively adapted our methods to meet the needs of our patients. We have been open to and have familiarized ourselves with the many other therapeutic approaches which we believe have made important contributions to the theory and practice of psychotherapy.

Indeed, we feel that all effective therapists use multi-disciplinary modes regardless of their basic systems and vary their personal style, pace and manner appropriately to the persons they are treating.

It was not until we immersed ourselves in the study of left/right brain research that we became aware of the degree to which all schools of psychotherapy express a bias, either in the direction of left-mode thinking/analyzing or right-mode feeling/expression. Left-mode therapies engage the patient in a process of talking, reasoning and interpreting past and present behavior. They stress the importance of insight in resolving neurotic conflict. Right-mode therapies encourage the patient to vividly re-experience old traumas in the here and now in order to surface repressed emotions which keep a person trapped in self-destructive patterns.

Sigmund Freud's early work included the uses of abreactive hypnosis which involved strong emotional expressions, but in the development of his therapy, he became uncomfortable with the powerful feelings it aroused. He replaced hypnosis with the more controlled method of free association. It is hardly surprising in view of his medical background and logical scientific bent that he created a largely left/brain therapy.

Many of Freud's former followers rebelled against his theories and created right/brain therapies. Among these thinkers was Carl Jung who challenged Freud's concept of the unconscious as the dark chaos of impulse. Rather, he postulated the collective unconscious as a spiritual haven of a shared human heritage. Wilheim Reich emphasized the importance of the body as a repository of repressed emotions. Fritz Perls, the founder of Gestalt Therapy, went on to take the extreme position that all "talking about" and interpretations were worthless, that the only useful therapy came from awareness and experiencing.

All the psychological theories that developed since Freud's contribution can be viewed as loosely falling into two major categories: The left mode which emphasizes thinking, talking and analysing and the right mode which stresses feelings, expression and action.

Left Mode	Right Mode
Psychoanalysis	Gestalt
Rational Emotive	Primal
Transactional Analysis	Bio-energetic
Reality Therapy	Psycho Drama
Family Therapy	Implosive

All of these therapy systems are directed toward the ultimate integration of thinking and feeling even though each approaches the task from an initial left-or right-mode position. Many of the aforementioned therapies allow for the opposite mode as a secondary emphasis.

Psychologists have long been aware of the basic neurotic types that polarize into the obsessive-compulsive/paranoid and the hysteric/impulsive personalities. All therapies are familiar enough with these mal-adaptive behaviors but none have been able to adequately explain what factors dispose a given person to develop a particular form of symtoms.

Dr. David Shapiro in his brilliant work, *Neurotic Styles*, which has become a classic in the field of dynamic psychiatry and ego-psychology, holds that a person's mode of thinking and perception creates a matrix from which various traits, systems and defense mechanisms crystallize. He also noted that intellectual inclinations, vocational aptitudes and social affinities have a certain connection with thinking and perceiving style.

"We are not surprised," he says, "to hear that a bookkeeper or a scholar has developed an obsessional type of neurosis or that a woman who came to psychotherapy because of severe emotional outbursts is an actress who is a bright and vital social companion but is uninterested in and rather uninformed about science or mathematics!"

Although this book was written before the advent of split-brain research, Dr. Shapiro's explorations into the dicotomy of behavioral styles contributed to an understanding of left/right brain personality dominance.

A review of the psychological literature fails to uncover any report which makes a direct connection between a person's brain dominance and his characteristic way of responding to life situations.

We believe that the right/left brain dominance factor determines whether a person will be predisposed toward the obsessive-compulsive/paranoid or hysteric/impulsive personality style. And for each person the particular admixture of right/left brain qualities coupled with their early child/parent interactions and personal experiences account for the many variations of perceptual style which determine how a person conducts his life.

People find it surprising that some children are drawn to an aunt, uncle or close family friend more intensely than to their own parent.

We believe, all other things being equal, that the lack of affinity that disturbs the primal bond might well be a clash of brain-style dominance. In the atmosphere of the extended family, there is always someone available who mirrors the child's left- or right-mode perception. In today's more isolated childrearing environment, most children are raised by two, or in many cases a single parent and the likelihood of perceptual mismatches is greatly increased. It is not uncommon for parents and grown children to confess, ''We never did seem to be on the same wavelength,'' or ''I could never feel really close to my mother/daughter.''

In a hyperthetical case of a left-brain child and a right-brain mother, let us assume that the child had his first brush with racial or ethnic persecution. The probable response of the right-brain mother would be to comfort and support the child by reassuring him that she loves him and by actively protesting the incident. The left-brain child would be unsatisfied by this approach and would benefit more from a detailed explanation of the meanings behind the experience. Had the child been a right-brain dominant like the mother, he would have found her response gratifying.

If the same incident had involved a right-brain child and a left-brain mother, the result might have been equally unfulfilling. Offering verbal explanations to a right-brain child in place of hugging and reassurances of love would not answer the needs of the child.

The existence of a parent/child brain dominance mismatch is quite common and probably contributes significantly to developmental difficulties in childhood.

The left-dominant child with right-dominant mother will often feel misunderstood, detached and isolated since his tendency is to make sense of the world through ideas and concepts which may not be mirrored by the right-brain parent.

The right-dominant child with the left-dominant mother will have trouble trusting feelings in himself and others and often feels unloved and lonely. The left-brain mother's emphasis on conceptualizing and explaining the logical reasons for most interactions usually leaves the child confused and unvalidated.

When the brain dominance factor is shared between parent and child, however, the child is more likely to feel understood and loved.

Where both the parent and child are left dominant, communication will be with words, ideas and concepts. The child will feel understood and validated when he can verbalize his thoughts with the parent.

Where the right mode is shared by parent and child, most interactions will be with feelings, touching, body language and art. The child will feel loved and validated. The atmosphere in these relationships is also lighter since the parent can better appreciate the child's behavior.

Although *love* and *understanding* are the very building blocks of all human psychological development, there is a subtle but significant distinction between the way the left- and right-dominants internalize these two qualities.

The left-dominant child is more likely to feel *understood* or *misunderstood* as an initial response in a relationship.

The right-dominant child will initially respond to feeling *loved* or *unloved*.

Love and understanding are important to both types but with a preference of emphasis for each.

It is our belief that when a child's dominant perceptual brain style is mirrored by a parent or other important caretaker, there will be a greater tendency toward left/right balance. Growing up in an atmosphere of acceptance and affirmation of his basic perception, the child develops the self-confidence to explore his other less accessible side.

There is an interesting analogy between the above experience and that of successful psychotherapy. One of our first tasks upon meeting with a new psychotherapy client is to assess where they are situated on the left/right dominance range. Perception is primary to making sense of personal experience and we believe that no effective therapeutic change can take place unless the therapist and the client can make contact on a level of shared reality.

As we commented earlier, all therapy systems have a left/right bias which is seldom acknowledged. A mismatch between therapy systems and client could be equivalent to a parent/child mismatch and have the similar result of leaving the client feeling misunderstood and unvalidated.

As an initial approach in psychotherapy, we believe the rational left-mode therapies, such as Psychoanalysis and Transactional Analysis which are content and insight oriented, are clearly appropriate for left brain dominant people and that the feeling right-mode systems, such as Gestalt and Bio-energetics are effective for right-brain people.

Our process in Phase I of this approach is to enter the world of the client with the therapeutic approach that mirrors his own perception. And so our work with the left dominant lawyer, accountant or engineer would be verbal, cognitive and interpretive. The methods we would employ with the right-brain musician, salesman or artist would come from any of the affective/feeling therapies.

Our first task is to make them aware of the legitimacy of their own perception and the behavior that follows from it. A great deal of the self doubts and the internalized criticisms from others that clients bring into therapy are directly related to a lack of clarity of their own nature.

As the client starts to understand and appreciate his own unique left/right dominant style, he begins to undertstand the important people in his life with whom he interacts. A familiarity with the personality dynamics of left/right brain dominance helps to remove the blaming of himself and others.

After a period of working with the therapy system which matches the client's own dominant style, during Phase I, we move into Phase II which involves a shift to the opposite side. By way of example, after initial use of cognitive-oriented therapy with a left-dominant accountant who has learned to deal with many of his problems by effectively using reason, logic and structured planning, we introduce one of the right-mode therapies such as Gestalt.

With a right-dominant artist, the switch would be from a right-mode therapy to a left-mode one.

During Phase II the left-dominant client will be asked the right-brain question: "How do you *feel* about that?" and the right-dominant will be asked the left-brain question: "What are you going to *do* about it?"

The left-dominant will be encouraged to develop more sensitivity to feelings and to trust his intuition. The right-dominant will be shown how being more organized and postponing gratification can enhance his life.

Phase III is briefly outlined in the following grouping of left/right brain process.

Phase I   *VALIDATING PERCEPTION*
*Using the appropriate left- or right-oriented therapy to match the dominance of the patient.

Phase II   *BRAINSWITCHING*
*Introducing the opposite therapy style in order to expand the patient's awareness of his less used or avoided side.

Phase III   *IMPLEMENTATION*
*This stage is more involved. It deals with the patient gaining additional *insight*, developing the *courage* to overcome specific fears, and finally taking *appropriate action*.
*Insight, courage and action are essential to the development of more growth-oriented patterns of living.

These factors listed under Phase III above surface during Phase I and Phase II and are discussed when appropriate, but they are primary areas of focus during the third phase.

It is our belief that some people seeking psychotherapy are over-laterized. This tendency for extreme dominance may be self-destructive.

Our experience is that the clients who successfully complete the three phases of therapy move toward greater whole brain balance. They retain their basic left/right dominance but with more acceptance of themselves.

The communication model we designed for Odd Couples, the three A's, works equally well as a process in individual psychotherapy.

Acceptance, Appreciation and Accommodation are the stages a client is guided through in the course of treatment.

He *accepts* his own brain dominant style.

He *appreciates* his own style and the opposite style in others.

He *accommodates* to the less dominant side within himself.

In these ways he moves toward greater balance.

Many patients develop increased clarity of their thinking style and gain more control over their lives when the Odd Couple Theory is shared by the therapist.

Whatever the psychological orientation of the psychotherapist, the use of left/right perceptual understanding and technique has an important place in the treatment process.

The following case history·of a young man named John will illustrate how the left/right brain approach is used to help the client better frame the nature of his conflict.

John came into therapy with complaints of feeling depressed, confused and of being unable to make decisions in his relationships. His mother was an overpowering figure in his life who ran the family business. She made many demands on him which he found difficult to fulfill. His father was a passive man with artistic abilities which were never developed. He worked in the family business and deferred to his wife. He died when John was in his late teens.

John, who is in his early thirties, left an unhappy relationship with a woman with whom he lived for three years. He left her one year ago and finds himself unable to separate from her emotionally and is considering a reconciliation.

John is an intelligent, sensitive man who like his father has not developed a work life appropriate to his talents and interests. He has a decided right brain dominant outlook.

For the first few months of therapy the treatment plan consisted primarily of the Gestalt approach to eliciting deep feelings through the use of experience-inducing techniques such as role-playing, guided imagery and focusing on body awareness. During this period, John had the opportunity to explore his life in a way that was consistent with his right dominant perceptual style. The process in Phase I not only validated his own reality, but helped to establish a high measure of trust between himself and the therapist.

Whenever a person has a neurotic problem, it is reflected in left/right brain confusion. In Phase II which we call "Brainswitching," this difficulty is addressed. This process makes the patient aware of how he perpetuates his conflict.

In the dialogue which follows this technique is used:

JOHN: Judy will never concede that she could be wrong about something. When she knows she's wrong, she usually changes the subject or says she doesn't want to talk about it any more. I'm always wanting to talk things out, to know how she feels, but she tries to reduce everything to black and white and gets angry when I try to discuss a problem.

THERAPIST: You must feel very frustrated. You want her to be more open with you. We've talked about this in the past but I'd like you to tell me all the other things that bother you about Judy and how they make you feel.

JOHN: Well, she's very moody. I can never be sure how she will be when I call her. First I feel guilty, as if I'm responsible when she is depressed, then I feel I have to make it up to her and I'm always left feeling that I did something wrong. Then she's not very stimulating to be with. She's not interested in art the way I am. All she likes is watching soap operas. Also she's very possessive, wants to know where I am all the time. It makes me feel like I have to account to her. I never felt free when I lived with her. I felt that she never really trusted me.

THERAPIST: How about the closeness and the warmth that you feel was lacking?

JOHN: She was always hugging me, and holding hands and telling me to drive carefully and would call me at the office to see if I was O.K. but I never really felt comfortable with all that. It was more like she was treating me like her child than her lover. Occasionally, the sex was good but mostly she was too tired or angry with me.

THERAPIST: From your description of your relationship with Judy, one would think you would be happy to be separated from her.

What is it about Judy that causes you to feel that you want a reconciliation?

JOHN: I feel she loves me and I need that. I think she knows me better than anyone else and I can't seem to let go of her. I love her a lot...I don't know if I can go on without her!

When I'm away from her, I feel I want to be with her. My body actually aches. Many times during each day I have a longing to phone her. I'm managing to hold my calls to only once a day. I want to clear up my confusion before getting hooked in with her again.

(At this point the therapist introduces Phase II - Brain-switching. The process is designed to highlight the ambivalence the patient experiences.)

THERAPIST: Well, I recommend that you have to set a deadline of two weeks for a reconciliation with Judy.
(John is visably uncomfortable.)

JOHN: I don't *think* I could do that. There are just too many problems between us. I'll be right back to where I left off when I walked out. No, I don't *think* so.

THERAPIST: John, what did you experience when I told you that you had to set a deadline?

JOHN: I was shocked and was beginning to feel trapped again, but then when I considered the idea, I knew it was not what I wanted.

THERAPIST: Suspend your judgement for a few minutes and imagine that you are speaking to Judy. Tell her what you want from her...what you would need in order for you to move in with her.

JOHN: I have doubts as to whether she can give me what I want.

THERAPIST: Do it anyway.

JOHN: Judy, I really want to come back to you, but I must have more open communication with you. We have to work toward a more trusting relationship...I would like you to go into counseling with me.

THERAPIST: How is she reacting to that? What does she say?

JOHN: No! I won't go into therapy with you. You are just trying to prove you are right and that I have to change.

THERAPIST: How does that *feel* when you hear that?

JOHN Frustrating. Like it's hopeless.

THERAPIST: What do you want to *do* now?

JOHN: Tell her that it's over.

THERAPIST: Tell her.

JOHN: I don't think we have much of a future as a couple, Judy. I'd like to remain friends but I can't live with you.

THERAPIST: How does it *feel* when you say that?

JOHN: Sad. I *feel* kind of pushed down, depressed...

THERAPIST: What is the sadness about?

JOHN: Well, lots of memories. It's like losing all the good times we spent together. There were lots of those good times. Now I *feel* they are never going to happen again...like I'm losing a good friend.

THERAPIST: You are describing the dichotomy between your intellectual left brain and your feeling right brain. The feeling right brain is still saying, "But I have this strong bodily feeling for her." And your left brain is saying, "But it doesn't work. She doesn't understand me. She doesn't make me feel good. She irritates me when she's with me." The right brain says, "But I feel this terrible yearning for her. I can't leave her. I can't destroy what we had. Those beautiful feelings will never come again if I leave her."

The feelings in the body tend to remain static; they persist long after the time when the experiences actually existed. It's the job of the left brain to challenge these feelings. It says, "I know how you feel. You have this yearning but, look buddy, you're not going to kid me, because I understand the consequences, because if I rely on you, you'll just take me off the bridge into deep water and tell me how nice it feels to be falling down...until I hit the water!"

That's the kind of dialogue that you really have to develop within yourself, John.

There is nothing sacrosanct about your feelings. Your feelings are not going to give you a path to follow.

Your feelings will only give you craving for expression. They have no conscience; they have no forethought of the consequences of their actions. They are just your feelings.

You can change your feelings by having new experiences. So, in a sense, it's foolish to be trapped by your feelings because new feelings are being created all the time. Even though feelings present themselves as powerful and immovable, you have the capacity to change them.

JOHN: So, what do I do? It's easier for me to say I'm going to break it off than actually doing it. I'm still not sure that I'm capable of it.

THERAPIST: First you have to know that if you go against your feelings about wanting to be with Judy, you're going to have pain and longings. Your right brain is going to try to perpetuate your old feelings of longing. Your right brain is going to tell you that you can't leave or you will suffer so much your heart will break. But that's all nonsense.

Actually, you will encounter resistance to change, but you have a choice as to whether you will allow your resistance to prevail.

You need to focus on what you really want and what is actually possible. Once you get that down pat, you will be able to carry through. But continuing to serve your right brain, which is what you have been doing up to now, will only keep you stuck.

JOHN: I see that. I have to make up my mind to deal with my indecision.

THERAPIST: That's your left brain talking now! What's your right brain saying now?

JOHN: That I want to be with her and it's dangerous to be somewhere else. It's not safe, not comfortable, not easy. Then I worry about her being helpless, not being able to take care of herself.

THERAPIST:	And now your left brain answer?
JOHN:	I know she can take care of herself...that helplessness act is how she manipulates me.
THERAPIST:	What do you think it would take to recognize the manipulations when they occur?
JOHN:	I guess what happens when Judy tries to get me to do something I don't want to do is that my right brain takes over....O.K., instead of looking at the situation and thinking about it, I'll let myself be drawn into an argument and start defending myself or I'll go along with her to avoid an argument. Instead of saying this is what I want or don't want and insisting on a rational discussion, I allow her to suck me into arguing.
THERAPIST:	That's exactly right.

Instead of saying, "Hey, wait a minute, what's going on here? *Think! Think!* I've got to stay awake in my left brain.

It takes courage to move into your left brain and act on what logic tells you while your *feelings* are looming up with impending disaster.

She might tell you she doesn't love you any more. She might say I don't need you any more, get out of my life. How could you live without her? Could you survive that? Doesn't it feel like a matter of life and death?

That's the ultimate power of the right brain—to make it feel like not following its dictates is a matter of life and death.

So, of course, it takes courage to stand against the emotional tide.

Your right brain is saying you can't make it if this woman cuts you off, but if you listen to your left brain, you will hear, "John, it's not a matter of life and death. If you remain on your own, you will survive and you will find other people to be with and you will find a way to be happy." |

JOHN:	I know what you're saying about courage because I usually know what I should do but I get scared and then I get confused and then I get lost in my *feelings*.
THERAPIST:	Exactly. You won't let yourself know because it's too scary to act on it. So the real challenge is to continue to let yourself know and to develop the courage to do what is good for you.

The process in Phase II helps the patient understand his confusion, ambivalence and indecisiveness.

The left/right brain technique of switching back and forth expands the consciousness of the patient and creates a concrete structure for him to understand his choices.

John became practiced at recognizing the ways in which he contributed to his own confusion and inaction in many areas of his life. He explored his worklife and the seemingly insoluble problem of his relationship with his mother. John's inability to separate emotionally from his mother was reflected in his difficulty in leaving his dead-end job and ending his destructive relationship with Judy.

Implementation: The main ingredients of Phase III are insight, courage and action. When a person becomes acutely aware of the dynamics of the left/right brain process within his personality, he starts to realize that the major block to changing his destructive pattern is fear of loss.

All effective psychotherapy deals with the classic issues of separation and individuation. Whether the psychological orientation is Psychoanalysis or Gestalt, developing the patient's level of self-awareness and self-love is basic to his recovery.

Intrinsic to self-love is the realization that one can stand alone; that no one at the deepest level needs any other person in order to be happy; and that manipulation of others, or by others, is unnecessary and counter-productive to personal growth.

This developed sense of self is the foundation in Phase III for confronting one's fears. Nevertheless, our fears are generally deep rooted and we require a hefty dose of courage to follow through on our intentions to act. It is through the process of acting upon our enlightened intentions that our inner hopes are realized and our self-esteem is enhanced.

John continued to struggle in his relationship with Judy. Eventually he began to see how his indecisive behavior was a mask for his fears which were perpetuating his unhappy life. As John gained more positive feelings about himself, he developed the courage to make a complete break with Judy. He has been able to relate to his mother in a new way which has fostered an atmosphere of mutual respect and he is now facing his long submerged issue of career change.

Had John been a left dominant rather than a right dominant, the treatment plan would have had the opposite sequence:

Phase I would have emphasized cognitive left oriented therapy.

Phase II would have introduced right brain therapy into the process in order to create the *brainswitching* experience.

Just as the right-dominant gets stuck in dealing with his left brain perception, left-dominants usually have trouble allowing and negotiating their right-brain *feelings*. Right-dominants must learn to listen to their left cognitive side if they want to improve the structure and productiveness of their lives. And left-dominants must open to their right brain sensitivity and intuition in order to have warmer relationships and more inner peace.

It is our sincere hope that the Odd Couple Theory will serve to inform, inspire and stimulate other professionals to explore their views of psychotherapy and contribute to the ongoing dialogue regarding the nature of human personality.

afterword

It was our intention when we decided to write The Odd Couple Syndrome to reach a broad strata of readers.

Had we geared the book solely to a lay audience, we might have included more cartoons, anecdotes and personal stories. Had we intended to reach a largely professional readership, we would have developed the theorectical portion of the work in greater detail.

It is our hope that we have succeeded in blending these two approaches into an interesting, entertaining and thought-provoking book.

We feel that the issues and ideas we have presented have practical application value for improving everyday life.

There is also the opportunity for psychologists and other mental health professionals to consider the far-reaching implications of left/right brain personality theory.

The authors would like to engage all our readers in an open forum of ideas, concepts, speculations, personal experiences and humorous stories about neat and sloppy styles.

We believe that an exchange of this kind will provide new insights into this emerging study of human behavior.

All correspondence may be addressed to the authors:

Selwyn Mills
Max Weisser
90 Schenck Avenue
Great Neck, NY 11021

NOTES

1. Seymore Fisher, M.D.; *Scientific Credibility of Sigmund Freud* p. 138, R.P. Greenberg, 1977.
2. Ibid. p. 146.
3. Ibid. p. 148.
4. David Kensey and Marilyn Bates; *Character and Temperament Type* (Solona Beach, CA.) Promethues Books, 1978, p. 3.
5. Charles Hampden-Turner; *Map of the Mind* (New York) Collier Books; 1981; p. 44.
6. Jack Fincher; *The Brain*; Washington, D.C., U.S. News Books; 1980, p. 25.
7. Betty Edwards; *Drawing on the Right of the Brain*; Los Angeles; J.P. Tarcher; 1979; p. 29.
8. R.E. Gur & R.C. Gur; *Lateralization in the Nervous System*; Academic Press; 1977.
9. Vandim Deglin; "Split Brain" *The Unesco Courier*; January, 1976; pp. 5–32.
10. Jerre Levy; "Cerebral Asymmetries as Manifested in Split-Brain Man"; *Hemisphere Functions in the Human Brain*; John Wiley; 1974.
11. John Seamon; "Coding and Retrieval Process and the Hemispheres of the Brain"; *Hemisphere Functions in the Human Brain*; John Wiley; 1974.
12. Thomas Blakeslee; *The Right Brain*; Garden City, NY; Doubleday 1980; p. 174.
13. Jerre Levy, IBID
14. Richard Restak, M.D.; *The Brain: The Last Frontier*; NY; Doubleday; 1979; p. 183.
15. Thomas Blakeslee, IBID, p. 179.

BIBLIOGRAPHY

Blakeslee, Thomas R. *The Right Brain*. N.Y. Doubleday, 1980.

Deikman, Arthur, M.D. *The Observing Self*. Boston, Beacon Press 1982.

Edwards, Betty. *Drawing on the Right Side of Brainn*. Ca. J.P. Tarcher 1979.

Evatt, Cris & Feld, Bruce. *The Givers and the Takers*. N.Y. Macmillian Publishing 1983.

Fincher, Jack. *The Lefties*. N.Y. G.P. Putman, 1977.

Fisher, Seymour. *Scientific Credibility of Sigmund Freud*. N.Y. Basic Books, 1977.

Gazzaniga, Michael. *The Integrated Mind*. Y.Y. Plenum Press, 1978.

Huron, Jennine. *Neuropsychology of Left-handedness*.

Houston, Jean. The Possible Human. Los Angeles, Ca. J.P. Tarcher, 1983.

Kopp, Sheldon. *Even a Stone can be a Teacher*. J.P. Tarcher, 1985.

Keirsey, David & Bates, Marilyn. *Please Understand Me*. Ca. Prometheus, 1978.

Leonard, George. *The Silent Pulse*. N.Y. E.P. Dutton, 1978.

Loye, David. *The Sphinx and the Rainbow*. Colorado New Science Books, 1983.

Restak, David. *The Brain The Last Frontier*. N.Y. Doubleday, 1979.

Sagan, Carl. *The Dragons of Eden*. N.Y. Ballatine Books 1977.

Segalowitz, Sid, J. *Two Sides of the Brain*. Prentice-Hall, 1983.

Shapiro, David. *Neurotic Styles,* Basic Books, 1965

Smith, Edward. *The Growing Edge of Gestalt Therapy,* N.J. Citadel Press, 1977.

Stock, Rip. *Odd Couple Mania*. Ballantine Books. N.Y. 1983.

Springer-Deutch. *Left Brain, Right Brain*. Ca. Freeman Co. 1981.

Turner, Hampden Charles. *Maps of the Wind*. N.Y. Macmillian Publishing, Co. 1982.

Virshup, Evelyn. *Right Brain People in a Left Brain World*. Ca. Guild of Tutor Press, 1978.

Donovan, Pricilla. *Whole-Brain Thinking*. William Morris Co. 1984.

Zdenek, Marilee. *Right Brain Experience*. McGraw-Hill Book Co., 1983.

INDEX

GLOSSARY

We have attempted to avoid the use of technical terms in this book wherever possible in order to facilitate a smooth flow of ideas.

However, we believe the definitions of terms and concepts in this glossary may prove helpful to the reader unfamiliar with writings in the field.

For readers who would like to pursue further study in left/right research, we have included explanations of terminology commonly used in medical and psychological sources.

AAA:
Acceptance, Appreciation and Accommodation - a system for resolving interpersonal conflict.

ADDICTIVE BEHAVIOR:

excessive drinking, over-eating, drug-abusing, gambling and romantic fusion appear to be related to right-brain process. For example, impulsive, gratification-seeking, risk-taking and sensation responsive traits.

ALEXITHYMIC:

a person who functions almost completely through the left brain (OCSRS - Extreme Left #1, page 55).

APHASIA:

impairment or loss of ability to articulate words or to comprehend speech.

ATTITUDE VS PERCEPTION:

attitudes are shaped by learned social
roles and environmentally conditioned
experience. Perception is created by a
style of thinking about and experiencing
reality.

BORDER HARMONY:

a relationship between two left-brain
dominants or two right-brain dominants,
usually characterized by acceptance and
cooperation rather than the control and
competition of many Odd Couple relationships.

BRAIN STEM:

the lower portion of the brain at the core
which includes the pons and the medula.

BROCA'S AREA:

exists in the left hemisphere, lower
middle portion - vital to speech produc-
tion.

CEREBELLUM:

a round mass which rests under the rear
of the cerebral cortex which is attached
to the spinal cord. It attends to the
balance of the body and automatic motor
sequences like running.

CEREBRAL CORTEX or CEREBRUM:

the surface layers of the cerebral hemispheres. It is called gray matter because
its many cell bodies give it a gray
appearance in contrast to the nerve fibers
that make up the white matter.

146

CEREBRAL HEMISPHERES:

two large masses of nerve cells and fibers
- the bulk of the brain. The two hemispheres are separated by a deep fissure
but connected by the corpus callosum.

COMMISSUROTOMY:

The cutting of the corpus callosum
between the left and right hemisphere of
the cerebral cortex.

CONFLICTING POLARITIES:

the classic Felix/Oscar relationship.
Also relates to the split within a single
person. One who is both very neat and
very sloppy at different times.

CONVERGING POLARITIES:

an odd couple relationship where each person leans toward the center. See OCSRS.
Each person is open to the different style
of the other.

CORPUS CALLOSUM:

a massive bundle of neural fibers connecting the left and right hemispheres of the
cerebral cortex which permits the two
halves to communicate directly with one
another.

CRAFTSPEOPLE AND ARTISTS:

Craftspeople think out a problem step by
step, assemble materials, research methods
of approach and then proceed to work.
Most Artists start with an inspiration,
an image or some intuitive feeling, without having a precise plan. Craftspeople
tend to be left-brain dominants. Artists
are generally right-brain dominants.

DICHOTIC LISTENING:

>a testing procedure designed to determine hemispheric preference by transmitting simultaneous data to both ears.

DOMINANT HEMISPHERE:

>the side of the brain that controls the information processing of a particular task.

EEG (electroencepholograph):

>a device which records electrical activity in the brain. During spatial tasks such as doing block design test, the right brain is more active. Reading and writing activate the left brain.

EPILEPSY:

>a condition in which the brain produces an intermal electrical discharge. A minor seizure may not be noticeable, whereas a major seizure may cause muscle contractions and unconsciousness.

HEMISPHERECTOMY:

>a surgical operation to remove the left or right side of the cerebral cortex.

HEMISPHEREIC LATERALIZATION:

>specialization of the two cerebral hemispheres with regard to function.

IMAGES:

>Left Brain - the optical image of external objects received by the visual system and interpreted by the brain.
>Right Brain - a visual representation of something not present to the senses from the environment.

KINESTHETIC DOMINANT:

one who responds on a sensorial level primarily to what one feels.

LATERAL THINKING:

looking at a problem from many angles rather than searching for a direct, head-on solution; concerned with the generation of new ideas; believed to be the natural style of the right brain.

LEFT - BRAIN DOMINANT:

one who favors the left-hemisphere thinking style in their behavior.

NEAT/SLOPPY BEHAVIOR:

the way in which one deals with their environment; the style by which one classifies, organizes, arranges, uses, maintains and cares for material objects.

NEUROLINGUISTIC PROGRAMMING:

a theory developed by Richard Bandler and John Grinder that all human communication styles are basically reducible to three sensory modes: Visual, Auditory and Kinesthetic.

OBSESSIVE-COMPULSIVE BEHAVIOR:

recurrent and persistent thoughts, ideas and repetitive, ritualized actions. Most common among extreme left-brain dominants.

ODD COUPLE SYNDROME:

> the theory that neatness and sloppiness
> are caused by a favored left-brain or
> right-brain style of perception. It is
> not attitude or neurosis, but a uniquely
> formed personal sensibility that is pri-
> marily responsible for neat/sloppy
> behavior.

ODD COUPLE SYNDROME RELATIONAL SCALE (page 55):

> a chart which gauges the left/right per-
> sonality types from moderate to extreme
> and indicates the kinds of relationships
> that are formed by their combination.

PERCEPTUAL DIFFERENTIAL DESIGN TEST (PDDT)p.43:

> a test to determine brain dominance based
> on black and white designs which corre-
> spond to left/right brain pattern prefer-
> ence.

RIGHT-BRAIN DOMINANT:

> one who favors the right hemisphere think-
> ing style in their behavior.

SAVERS AND THROWERS:

> Savers (accumulators) are people who
> become emotionally attached to objects
> and often suffer separation anxiety when
> discarding becomes an issue. Most savers
> are right-brain dominants.
> Throwers (discarders) are usually left-
> brained people who value function, organi-
> zation and aesthetic appearance more than
> attachment.

SPATIAL ABILITY:

> the ability to visualize and manipulate objects in space such as the skills involved in doing geometry and perspective drawing.

SPLIT-BRAIN EYE CHART TEST (page 92):

> a test for determining brain dominance. A right dominant person will grasp the message hidden in the mock eye chart more quickly than the left dominant because the right-brain sees whole patterns rather than details.

UNEVEN BALANCE:

> two neat or two sloppy people living together who unlike the "Border Harmony" type are competitive and controlling. In each pair the neater person is critical of the other. Usually it is a relationshp engrossed in power struggles.

VERTICAL THINKING:

> the use of a step-by-step method of logic; concerned with proving and developing concept patterns. In contrast to lateral thinking which is speculative, vertical thinking is analytical and believed to be a left-brain process.

WADA TEST:

> a test to determine the functions connected to a particular part of the brain. This is done by anesthetising only the left or the right side.

WERNICKE'S AREA:

> this section in the lower rear of the left hemisphere is associated with thought and language.